MW00638185

DREAM
DESIGN
LIVE

*To my parents, who taught me
to believe in the beauty of my dreams,
and to my dearest Fabian,
for encouraging me to chase them.
Thank you for your unwavering
love and support.*

PALOMA CONTRERAS
DREAM DESIGN LIVE

ABRAMS, NEW YORK

CONTENTS

Crisp white walls,
tall ceilings, and
details abound in this
airy living room.

INTRODUCTION

I'm not the type of decorator who knew her calling from the time she began experimenting with crayons. Tucked away in my childhood bedroom—white wicker furniture with bedding covered in pink cabbage roses—I dreamed of faraway places and a life filled with beauty.

My love of foreign cultures continued as I grew. In college, I studied Spanish and Italian. Upon graduating, I became a high school Spanish teacher. The job felt familiar but never quite fit—much like a sweater that looked okay but made me itch all over. I loved the subject matter and my rapport with the students, but I was restless.

After I'd been teaching for a few years, my husband, Fabian, and I traveled to Paris, Rome, and Florence. It was my first trip to Europe. Italy enchanted me—the architecture, the language, the food, the history, the art, the people—and I felt excited and energized. I wanted to hang on to that feeling for as long as possible. It was time to design the life that I wanted to live—the life that felt true to who I am at my core.

It was July of 2007 and the only blogs I knew were written by friends who had moved away and kept "journals" so that their friends and families back home could keep up with their adventures. The first few entries I wrote were personal essays about design inspiration and decorating, two subjects I'd always loved. We had recently purchased our first home and I was in full-on nesting mode. Entrenching myself in design brought back the feelings of excitement and sense of fulfillment I'd felt while in Italy.

A mix of graphic
art in various
frames punctuates
this family room.

My newfound focus on living the good life through decorating and design resonated with my readers. More and more people started reading my blog. I started getting some great press and the blog's number of visitors and page views spiked. Offers for freelance writing and social media consulting started coming in. As I posted pictures of the design projects I was working on in my own house, I started receiving requests for small decorating projects. The more I wrote about design and worked on my own decorating projects, the more I realized that my personal version of *La Dolce Vita* centered on interior design and decorating. I left my teaching job and never looked back.

Today, creativity is the driving force in my life and thankfully, my profession allows me to tap into it daily. It's no accident that my personal journey started in my bedroom, the place that was my own, where, surrounded by the floral fabric I'd helped pick out, I dreamed of a life filled with beauty.

During my time in the design industry, I've come to realize that la dolce vita starts at home because that's where we are our truest selves. Our homes can help us live the lives we want and can be tools for living. They can provide an environment where we can retreat from the rest of the world and set the stage for the type of life we want to live. When things look and feel good at home, this feeling serves as an impetus for living beautifully in other areas of our lives. However, the reverse can also be true. If a house is not set up to help you live your best life, then you may be missing out on opportunities. You may dream of hosting dinner parties, but if you haven't found the right dining table, it's unlikely that you'll actually be able to host anyone in your home. You may aspire to appear stylish and put-together, but if your closet is a mess, chances are, it will be nearly impossible to do so. Living beautifully requires intention and follow-through, but that doesn't mean that it will be difficult.

VREELAND MEMOS

IN PURSUIT OF BEAUTY · TIMOTHY WHEALON

TOM
FORD

DREAM

Every design project begins with inspiration. When starting a new project, my jumping off point can be anything from a beautiful fabric to the colors in a piece of art to the vibe of a favorite clothing store. Inspiration is literally everywhere; it surrounds us at every hour of every day, and it has the potential to be both amazing and completely overwhelming. The chapters in this section address where to find inspiration and I discuss some of my own design inspirations while showing you how to cull through your ideas to create a cohesive vision. The trick is to know how to tap into inspiration and transform it into something that serves your mission, whether it is designing an entire house or setting the table for a special dinner.

In our office,
everyone has their
own inspiration
board to express
what they are
gravitating toward.

CHAPTER ONE

FINDING INSPIRATION

I did not consciously realize during my journey that I had been following the path of inspiration all along. From the childhood bedroom and experiences that began to shape my appreciation for interiors to the trip to Europe that inspired me to deeply examine my life's purpose and eventually shift gears, inspiration has appeared in my life time and time again, serving as the impetus for many important choices. Whether I'm creating a space for myself or for a client, every project starts with inspiration. Finding a source of inspiration establishes a framework for my vision. It helps me find the road map that will ultimately take me from inspiration to implementation.

Looking for, finding, and committing to a vision is a key step because designing a space, whether it's large or small, requires making many decisions. Having a strong source of inspiration will help you make these decisions. When things get overwhelming and you come to a halt, or when you have to make difficult budgetary decisions, going back to your inspiration for the project can help to bring things back into focus and help you make the best choices.

(Left) In our client's foyer, a calming oceanscape creates a welcoming vibe. (Opposite) A glimpse into our client's living room from their light-filled foyer.

Inspiration can be anything from the color of a favorite dress to the texture of a natural element such as a seashell or piece of wood. The key is that it must evoke a strong emotional response. Start by thinking of what makes you happy. Don't worry about whether something is on trend or in style. Instead, find the things that bring you joy. Pay attention to how things make you feel and what you find yourself responding to. Inspiration can be anywhere. It can strike at any moment. I've been inspired by architectural details while walking down the street, by memories associated with the flavor of a food, or by ideas that come from listening to a song. These are varied sources of inspiration, but the common factor is that something in these experiences made me happy, brought me a sense of peace, or spurred a strong emotional connection. Sometimes the inspiration is fleeting, and I know that if I don't capture it somehow, I'll lose it the next day. Other times, an image will stay with me for years and I'll be able to think of that source of inspiration and immediately conjure up what I was feeling at that moment.

A series of framed de Gournay panels in my dining room. They make me happy each time I see them.

Think about experiences that you find moving or memorable. Did you recently attend an exceptionally fabulous party? What did you love about it? What did the hostess do to make her guests feel special? Pay special attention to how you feel when you find yourself in different environments. Did you recently enter a room that felt especially inviting or cozy? If so, why do you think that might have been? Were there beautifully arranged stacks of books? Did candles and lamps on dimmers light the room, rather than overhead lighting? Was there a particular smell as you walked from one space to the next? Or maybe you sat next to a well-dressed person on a plane and noticed the combination of colors and fabrics in their outfit and how their accessories played off the overall look. Experiences can be just as inspiring and formative when it comes to our style as pictures in magazines or individual objects such as paintings.

Once you open yourself up to evaluating your daily life, you'll start to see many things that inspire you. Try to break down each experience and think about why something is attractive to you and what it is that you feel. In this way, you'll start to understand what types of objects or experiences make you feel happy and how to draw on them as you create your own space.

HIGH SOCIETY   ASSOULINE

DOMESTIC ART   ASSOULINE

LUIS BUSTAMANTE INTERIORES   EDICIONES EL VISO

"For me, inspiration often feels like a moment of panic. I'll be struck by something that feels incredibly moving and it sparks the impetus for me to act upon it right away."

For me, inspiration often feels like a moment of panic. I'll be struck by something that feels incredibly moving and it sparks the impetus for me to act upon it right away. Whether it is an idea for a client's window treatment, a new product design, or even an idea for a book or blog post, I usually feel an unsettling sense of urgency to make it happen.

I tend to experience inspiration for my projects when I'm relaxed, or on vacation. Travel is endlessly inspiring. It is so easy to get lost in the beauty of a new place. No matter where you are, stop to take in the colors, details, and feelings of a new place. Going on a trip gives us the opportunity to shake things up and escape our regular routine, so we're more likely to really look around us and pay attention. When you're going from day to day in your usual rhythm, you are less likely to notice interesting, beautiful, or inspiring things because you are so entrenched in your daily habits that you become immune to your surroundings. Whenever I get away, even if only for a short period, leaving my familiar surroundings immediately focuses my attention on the new place. Even better, I find that I always return rested, refreshed, recharged, and ready to tackle creative projects and see things with fresh eyes.

While it isn't always possible to go away on a trip, the important lesson here is to practice looking for inspiration so that you see it when it arrives at your doorstep—whether you go out looking for it or it arrives on its own. A great alternative is to indulge in a Saturday afternoon in pursuit of inspiration. Visit a local museum or gallery or get lost in a marathon of foreign or classic films.

We also have the world at our fingertips thanks to blogs, social media, magazines, books, and films. Between Instagram and Pinterest alone, inspiring images, people, and places are just a click away. Once you start identifying what resonates with you in your mind's eye, you'll find everyday places such as your favorite restaurant or boutique can also be great sources of inspiration. Allow yourself to think about the things that inspire you beyond their intended purpose or usual parameters.

Just the other day, I was at a stone showroom in Houston, shopping for countertops for a client, and I found myself completely inspired by all of the exotic stones they had on display. The stones were too exuberant for me use in a traditional application for a client, but I found myself in awe of the fact that so many beautiful colors and patterns occur naturally occur in the Earth. Mother Nature is truly the most talented of all designers! I started to look at slabs of marble, quartzite, and semiprecious stones through a completely different lens. These weren't just countertop materials; they were works of art. I stopped thinking of these materials

as something utilitarian for a kitchen and just started appreciating their beauty. One day, inspired by this trip, I will put together a project where I hang a beautiful slab on a big, white wall and have an incredibly impactful piece that sets the tone for everything else in the space. The showroom experience was a good reminder to think about why I'm inspired by something without ruling it out as "not my taste" immediately. Remember to open your eyes to everything around you.

Kelly Wearstler, a designer who definitely has a very unique and identifiable point of view, likes to cull inspiration from her huge collection of books. She once told me, "I have over two thousand titles of rare, out of print, vintage, and contemporary books on everything from fashion and design to architecture and landscape art. It is the first place I go for inspiration." If you don't have quite this extensive of a library, a similar and effective creative exercise to help you identify your inspiration would be to open up a few magazines and tear out the pages that inspire you.

Once you get in the habit of identifying what resonates with you, you'll start to find inspiration everywhere, even everyday places like your favorite restaurant or boutique. Whether you devote a day to go to a museum, have a picnic in the park, or pursue inspiration via your chosen outlet of inspiration, spend a few hours in this way and you may be surprised by how energized you will feel the next day.

For our client's house in the Hamptons, I was inspired by the family's desire for a relaxing place to escape the chaos of the city.

A chic mix of materials and silhouettes in a client's living room.

CHANNELING INSPIRATION

After you've gathered images, details, memories, natural objects, or other sources of inspiration that speak to you, the next step is to step back and evaluate everything. Evaluating and editing your sources of inspiration might seem overwhelming at first, but it's simply a matter of training yourself to think through why you were attracted to something. For example, do you find yourself being drawn to one color in particular or the work of a specific designer over and over? What recurring themes or design elements do you find yourself consistently attracted to?

After I have evaluated my sources of inspiration, I usually begin the editing process. Because it can be easy to get overwhelmed with visual inspiration through social media and blogs, I make sure to edit before I start working on determining the inspiration or direction for any given project, whether it is a powder room design for a client or an outfit to wear to a wedding.

First, I find the image or thing that I feel most moved by and use it as the central factor for the project's inspiration. It could be anything from a fantastic pair of shoes to a great chair or a photograph of one of my style icons, such as Lee Radziwill or Kate Moss. Next, I pull additional images that feel like they are in line with the same overall look or mood that I'm envisioning for the task at hand. Then, in the case of designing a space, I start to add individual fabrics, finishes, and furniture pieces that evoke the same feeling until it the picture is complete, like a story that has layers and a beginning, middle, and end.

Lay all these items out and determine what the unifying thread is. How do they relate to each other and what mood do they evoke? Are you currently drawn to a dark, moody color palette and masculine pieces? Are you finding yourself pulled toward a glamorous destination and a feminine color story? As you begin to nail down what ties together the various elements you are drawn to, you'll notice things come into focus and you'll find your inspiration and the direction in which it wants to take you. You might find the exercise of putting together a mood board to be very helpful as you learn to channel your inspiration and determine your style. You can do it the old-fashioned way and pin magazine tearsheets and fabric swatches to a bulletin board, or you can do it digitally through a Pinterest board or a mood board in InDesign or PowerPoint. As you see your various sources of inspiration come together, your story will come to life!

(Left) My precious cockapoo, Tate, comes to the office with me everyday. *(Opposite)* A beautiful fabric or wallpaper often inspires the design of a room.

PALOMA CONTR...

INTERIOR DESIGN

SCHUMACHER
SINCE 1889

SAMUEL & SONS
PASSEMENTERIE

CLARENCEHOUSE

MERIDA

Fine Paints
of Europe

The Select C...

Abstract art, a brass
and Lucite coffee
table, and a touch of
tiger print came
together in this client's
living room.

A CONSTANT PROCESS

I've developed my style by constantly studying the details of the things to
which I am drawn as well as the work of people I admire. Being a voracious,
lifelong learner and constantly seeking inspiration, then working toward understanding that inspiration has expanded my knowledge of various decorative
elements and how they work together.

This practice has been incredibly important in establishing my own sense of
style. For instance, I love French Empire antiques and I love the grand Georgian
and Greek Revival houses of the South. From analyzing my reactions to these
sources of inspiration, I have come to consider my aesthetic to be a modern take
on traditional style. As you begin to ask yourself questions about the things you
are drawn to, don't stress if you don't have all of the answers right away. The
wildly creative Jonathan Adler once told me, "I always keep my eyes and my
mind wide open. Creativity is an audacious undertaking and I try not to think
about it too much."

In the end, inspiration is about finding the bigger picture and helping yourself to understand the elements you need to create that picture. I don't think
it's possible to be overly inspired, but it's true that if you're working on a specific
project, you must edit. In order to have great style, you must learn to be a fierce
editor and stay faithful to what resonates most with you, then commit to building
on that vision as you go through the design process. This is truly the first step
to creating and living la dolce vita.

A mix of patterns
and materials
makes my guest
bedroom feel cheerful
and welcoming.

CHAPTER TWO

CREATING YOUR SIGNATURE STYLE

D o you follow certain accounts on social media or admire the work of specific designers who seem to have a signature style all their own, from their design work to their wardrobes to the way they entertain? Whether you have a business to promote or are just developing your personal style, having a well-defined, identifiable point of view creates brand recognition, as it were. Understanding your core aesthetic and being faithful to it cultivates a sense of authenticity to others and fulfillment within yourself because every decision or selection is in line with your signature style.

It may seem daunting to achieve a look that is all your own, but it is simply a matter of being in tune with yourself and embracing your favorite things. In the end, it is about being faithful to your own taste. After all, if you truly love something, it never really goes out of style. You may find that you have an appreciation for disparate styles, like I do. It is completely okay to like a lot of different things. I can certainly relate. Some days my mood is more modern, while other days I may be drawn to something ornate and over the top. As a matter of fact, if you were to look at several of my projects side by side, you'd notice that they each have their own look and vibe. Some tend toward modern, while others feature a more prominent use of color and pattern. However, they all have a unifying thread—they have been executed through my personal lens—which undoubtedly results in subtle similarities.

"In my case, I shy away from anything that feels too matchy-matchy, whether it is a set of furniture or a very one-dimensional color palette."

If I were to think about three designer friends with distinctive points of view, Mark D. Sikes comes to mind because he has carved out a niche for himself through his love of blue and white, classic American style, and stripes. Meanwhile, Alyssa Kapito, of the New York–based design firm Alyssa Kapito Interiors, has a distinct style that is clean, tailored, and composed of mostly neutral palettes. Finally, Suzanne Kasler's work is feminine and classical with European elements and soft color palettes. Chances are, they can all appreciate one another's work and are likely drawn to quite a few of the same things, but the execution and the lens through which their styles are filtered make them distinctly their own.

Despite what you may think, as a designer, I don't walk into someone's home and start picking it apart and identifying all of the mistakes. On the contrary, I certainly take in all of the details, but rather than looking for things to change, I look for clues into the personalities of the people who live there. The quirky things that speak to your personal story are the same elements that play into your personal style or "visual DNA." When working with new clients, I take these visual cues into account and find a way to accentuate the positive and improve upon any challenges. It gives us deeper insight into their likes and dislikes in order to formulate an original design for them.

If you find it challenging to describe your style or narrow down the things to which you gravitate the most, start by making a list of the things you dislike as a jumping-off point. Everyone can easily rattle off a list of things they definitely do not like! In my case, I shy away from anything that feels too matchy-matchy, whether it is a set of furniture or a very one-dimensional color palette. I also have a difficult time embracing chintz. I can certainly get behind a floral pattern used sparingly, but I just can't get on board with a floral explosion of pattern on pattern on pattern. Sometimes I think it is beautiful, but I could never live with it. It makes me physically uncomfortable because there is nowhere for my eye to rest. Now, it is your turn. What do you absolutely dislike? What would be unsettling for you to live with?

In my own bedroom, I've mixed my favorite ikat fabric with other elements I love: bamboo accents, gilt details, and abstract art.

Before you start narrowing down the individual elements that compose your personal style, think about how to determine how you would like your space to look, feel, and function. For instance, in my own house, I want rooms that look polished with a hint of glamour, but feel effortless and inviting. We really live in just about each room of our house, so it is important that every space is comfortable and lends itself to conversation whether we are entertaining a group of friends or it's just my husband and me hanging out at home.

I want each room to have some type of statement piece that truly speaks to my style. In my dining room, this is a series of six-foot-tall, framed de Gournay chinoiserie panels painted in white gold and aluminum on silk. In my powder room, it's the black-and-white cloud wallpaper. Each room should have a striking "wow" moment, yet it should work cohesively with the overall story of your home. Every individual room should complement the next, but before we can delve into how to do that, let's work on how to pinpoint your visual DNA.

"The foundation of each and every space I design is traditional because in my eyes, traditional style is the most enduring and it speaks to me on a very personal level. It resonates with me at my core."

Start thinking about the design elements you are most often attracted to. With these pieces in mind, what three words would you use to describe your personal style? I would say that my style is classic, glamorous, and effortless. My point of view is classic because my style and the design elements I love most are rooted in a traditional aesthetic. The foundation of each and every space I design is traditional because in my eyes, traditional style is the most enduring and it speaks to me on a very personal level. It resonates with me at my core. I then layer in various pieces that infuse the overall look with a bit of fresh, modern style to create a look that is all my own. My aesthetic is also glamorous because I love beautiful things. I love feminine silhouettes, metallic accents, statement pieces, and playing with scale. Lastly, and perhaps most importantly, my aesthetic is informed by my desire for every space that I touch to retain an effortless quality. In my opinion, the most beautiful rooms aren't just filled with pretty things, but they are also personal and inviting. After all, what good is a stunning room that is completely impersonal or whose contents are so precious that even the most well-mannered visitor feels like a bull in a china shop?

DEFINITION OF STYLE

Martyn Lawrence Bullard

"MY STYLE IS ALWAYS ECLECTIC. I NEVER LOVE ONE THING, I LOVE MANY THINGS . . . I NEVER HAVE A FAVORITE PERIOD OR DESIGN BECAUSE I BELIEVE THAT WOULD CORNER MY CREATIVE MIND. IT'S ALL IN THE MIX ANYWAY. ECLECTIC, YET ABLE TO EDIT AND STREAMLINE . . . THAT'S MY STYLE!"

Suzanne Kasler

"My style is marked by unexpected juxtapositions, a European sensibility. I love to mix high and low—casual elegance—and a focus on the architecture and the space."

Kelly Wearstler

"I want to take risks. My aesthetic is raw and refined. Colorful. Always something old and something new. Masculine and feminine. A mix of important history and fresh contemporary voices. The tension between opposites is sexy."

Alexa Hampton

"My style is eclectic. However, I am drawn to classic forms, and I prefer logical spaces to impractical ones. Interiors that combine great beauty with livability are always the goal."

Jesse Carrier & Mara Miller

"OUR STYLE IS A MIX OF CLASSIC DECORATING PRINCIPLES MIXED WITH ARTFUL PLACEMENT AND UTILITY. WE LET FURNITURE AND DECORATING SCHEMES EVOLVE AROUND A NARRATIVE, OR BUILD OFF ONE KEY IDEA OR ITEM—WHETHER IT IS A WELL-LOVED TABLE, PAINTING, OR EXCITING WALLPAPER."

Darryl Carter

"I am prone to marrying things that are highly classical together with very linear modern. I think together these create the perfect counterbalance, and avoid an otherwise uninteresting monolith of sameness. This would be my firm's ethos—we are very purposeful in our effort to create timeless rooms."

Kristen Buckingham

"It's definitely personal; I love a beautiful space with a sense of collected elegance, but it has to have livability and humor. Also edgy, not overtly feminine."

Madeline Weinrib

"MY HOME, THE WAY I DRESS, AND MY DESIGNS ALL TAKE INSPIRATION FROM DIFFERENT ERAS AND PLACES. I LOVE THE TIMELESS AND CLASSIC. YET I ALSO LOVE CONTEMPORARY. AND I ADORE THE UNIQUE AND ETHNIC PIECES I FIND ON MY TRAVELS."

WHAT IS YOUR INDISPENSABLE DESIGN ELEMENT?

Victoria Hagan
"Courage."

Beth Webb
"A LITTLE SOMETHING WITH PATINA IN EVERY ROOM. THAT, AND TEXTURE, TEXTURE, TEXTURE!"

Meg Braff
"Chinoiserie pieces, Lucite, and rattan are appropriate in almost every space."

Kate Rheinstein Brodsky
"Comfort! Small tables to put your drink on, throws to curl up under, a chair to read in, and flattering light!"

Suzanne Tucker
"Something old . . . [I like to] have at least one piece in a room with some age to it."

Alyssa Kapito
"Good proportions are everything."

Lauren Liess
"SOMETHING SCULPTURAL IN EVERY ROOM."

Ann Mashburn
"White paint."

Carolyne Roehm
"BLUE-AND-WHITE PORCELAIN."

Jonathan Adler
"A chandelier that is bigger than you think you need and more expensive than you think you can afford."

It is very important to me that my clients' homes reflect their styles more than mine, so the purest form of my personal style is what you will find in my own house or when I have a project such as a showhouse, when I can design for myself and not for a client. When you begin to tackle your own design project, pay close attention to the common threads or consistent ideas that you find yourself being drawn to time and time again. These are the things you truly love and are most in line with your signature style.

In order to get to the core of your aesthetic and weed out the things that you like, but don't love, ask yourself the following questions.

What color palette do you feel most comfortable with?

Now, which color do you find most interesting or beautiful?

Is there a general style that you find yourself drawn to most often?

Do you prefer traditional or modern?

Do you love a bold use of color and pattern or would you rather limit it to a few key pieces?

Do you like things that are elegant and ornate or do you prefer things that are rustic and refined?

Now, a key question: What piece or pieces in your home do you consider to be indispensable? Why?

Once you have narrowed down the things you like and dislike, as well as the three words you would use to describe your style, you can design your house, curate your wardrobe, and host events in your own unique, signature style. Having a well-defined, distinctive style that is all your own is important because it cultivates confidence, helps to make you or your brand more identifiable, and makes day-to-day life easier and more fulfilling because every selection is in line with your core aesthetic. The joy that you will derive from being surrounded by things that you love and that have personal meaning will extend into other facets of your life. Your personal style is a way to show the world exactly who you are at your core without having to utter a single word. While there are general guidelines, there are no rules in decorating. There is only good taste. When it comes to your home, your taste is what counts. If you love it, go for it. Life is too short not to!

DESIGN

Once you have a better understanding of your personal style, it is time to delve into the design process. It may seem daunting with so many decisions to be made, but ultimately, good design is about how all of those decisions—the individual pieces—come together to tell your story. From the overall mood of the room to the furniture placement in the space to the color palette and fabric selections, each of these decisions will help to set the stage for your design. These foundational elements of design are incredibly important because their purpose is to anchor the space you are designing. I'll guide you through the process of making design selections so that you can create your own version of la dolce vita at home, setting the stage for your personal story to be told.

Chinoiserie elements
and a classic
color palette make
this client's living
room feel timeless.

CHAPTER THREE

SETTING THE STAGE

One of the first questions I ask clients is what mood they would like for their space to reveal. It may seem like an odd question, but well-designed rooms are about so much more than just aesthetics. They make you feel welcome, happy, inspired, and so on. Think about the way you would like for your space to feel. Do you envision it as an informal space? Then it should feel cozy and inviting. Do you prefer to create a formal environment? In that case, the aim should be to create a polished and refined space. The questions go on from there—should the space lean more masculine or feminine, modern or traditional, or is it a mix of all of these options?

An important thing to keep in mind is the architecture of the space. You can incorporate modern elements into a room with very traditional moldings and millwork to achieve an eclectic, more modern-leaning environment, but it would feel inauthentic to have only clean-lined, ultra-modern furnishings in a house with classically traditional architecture. The sooner you pick a lane and stick with it, the sooner you'll be on your way to creating a space that looks and feels fantastic. Honor your home's architecture by playing up its attributes and being honest with yourself about what makes sense for the bones of the house. In the end, the result will look and feel much more genuine and cohesive.

"Think about the colors that look flattering on you. If a blue shirt looks fabulous with your coloring, chances are, you'll look stunning in a blue room!"

COLOR THEORY

Once I have established the mood and general design concept for a space, my next step is to determine the color palette. Different colors can create different moods. Some colors such as gray, black, brown, and darker shades of blue can read as moody or masculine, while white, ivory, pastels, and lighter shades of blue and green are considered soothing or cheerful. Think about the colors that look flattering on you. If a blue shirt looks fabulous with your coloring, chances are, you'll look stunning in a blue room! It might be helpful to start by thinking about your favorite colors and those that are completely off-limits in your mind. For instance, I personally love living in a house with white walls, which allows for my art and furnishings to really stand out. The effect is calm and soothing for both my husband and me, yet it has a great, graphic quality. I find that in my own house, I like a neutral foundation, accented with a few important colors—an anchor color, usually a neutral like a medium gray, to lend visual weight to the space. From there, I layer in accent colors. In my current home, I've used pink, blue, and chartreuse somewhat sparingly, but to great effect.

Some might argue that the use of bold color and pattern upon pattern in a space is more joyful than a room with a neutral palette and a few carefully selected touches of color and pattern. Personally, I find a lot of visual noise to be jarring, but when executed by someone who truly understands color and pattern, it can be fabulous. I have an appreciation for all types of design styles, but in the end, I am faithful to my own taste and what feels good to me, both inside and out.

Another thing to consider is what the upkeep of living with any particular color palette might be. For instance, I have white walls in my house, and my living room has white sofas and chairs. Because I love it and derive so much happiness from this look, I don't mind the fact that I have to lint-roll all of the upholstery in that room a couple of times a week to keep it looking fresh—and to keep it from driving me nuts! A more sane person, or one with young children, might not find that living with a white color palette is worth the upkeep and would opt for something more user-friendly.

Pillows made with a couple of my favorite fabrics add a hint of pattern to my living room.

Oval Room Blue by
Farrow & Ball,
a dusty blue-green,
stands out in
a client's nursery.

"Grays and whites are especially tricky, as undertones can read too blue, too green, or even mauve."

Just as the overall style and mood should be cohesive for the entire house, it helps to have a unifying thread for the spaces in a house, so that it all flows beautifully. While it is totally okay for the color palette in your home to vary a bit from one room to the next, I would urge you to keep the overall color palette somewhat consistent. If you have the urge to embrace a bold color somewhere, use it in a space that is separated from other spaces such as a bedroom, library, or powder room.

The best approach for having a cohesive color palette is to select an anchor neutral that works in every room of the house as well as using the same accent color repeatedly in the majority of the spaces. You can layer in these unifying colors through upholstery and pillow fabrics, rugs, draperies, artwork, and of course, wallcoverings and paint.

Finally, remember not to fret when it comes to paint! More than any other design element, paint requires some trial and error, but it is generally painless. Even when I know specific paint colors that I'd like to see in a space, I remind the client that we have tested the colors in the actual space, and the choices we make aren't written in stone. Lighting—both natural and artificial—can make colors vary tremendously from the way they appear in a paint deck, so I like to pick out a few similar shades, paint some swatches side by side, and wait twenty-four hours to make a decision so that we can see how the color looks as the light changes throughout the day. Grays and whites are especially tricky, as undertones can read too blue, too green, or even mauve. This experiment always yields a clear winner!

Cole & Son's exuberant Hummingbirds wallpaper serves as the joyful backdrop for this client's nursery.

WALL TREATMENTS WITH PERSONALITY

Some rooms present the opportunity to go beyond the ordinary and do something truly interesting on the walls besides paint. Specialty finishes such as lacquer, upholstered walls, and wallpaper are ideal for the more formal rooms in one's home that don't get frequent use, or for small spaces such as a vestibule or powder room, that won't get overwhelmed by such patterns. The high sheen of a true lacquer application adds instant glamour and truly elevates a space. We recently lacquered a client's library in the most beautiful shade of gray-blue. The result is stunning, but be advised that a true lacquer application is a tedious and expensive process. You'll want to hire a painter who is experienced in this technique because it is labor intensive and requires multiple coats of painstakingly applied paint. Plus, the ultra reflective finish reveals every last imperfection, so walls must be perfectly smooth. It's definitely not a DIY project or for the faint of heart.

For a more attainable way to dress up your walls, turn to wallpaper. I usually wallpaper at least one room in every client's home. Solid-colored wallpapers made of grass cloth or hemp are a great way to infuse subtle texture into a space, while patterned wallpapers provide an opportunity for injecting personality into a room and can be a great outlet for experimenting with scale. Don't forget to ask your installer to wrap your outlet covers and light switches in your wallpaper as well for a truly custom, seamless look!

**Best Rooms for
Showstopping Walls:**
- Entry
- Powder Room
- Closet Interior
- Library
- Guest Bedroom
- Guest Bathroom

A wallpaper by
Katie Ridder sets the
stage for the
mix of textiles in this
client's bedroom.

(*Below*) Grasscloth wallpaper adds texture to these pretty powder rooms. (*Opposite*) Cole & Son's Fornasetti Nuvolette Cloud wallpaper adds a graphic punch to my powder room.

BEST-LAID PLANS

After I have determined the color palette for each room, I move on to the floor plan. I start by figuring out all of the individual furniture pieces that we will need for each room and then make specific selections. In our office, we do professional floor plans and furniture layouts in AutoCAD or SketchUp so clients can see how all of the furnishings will work in relation to one another in scale, but you can easily lay it all out on graph paper. As you begin plotting out your room, consider how you'll use the space and what the focal point will be. For instance, in a living room, the focal point is typically the fireplace. If you'd like your living room to reveal a formal mood, you might select a beautiful painting to place above the fireplace. If the mood you're seeking is more casual and you plan to have informal gatherings watching the big game with friends or binge-watching your favorite show on Netflix, chances are that your TV will be the focal point. Another thing to keep in mind is the flow of traffic, making sure that there is plenty of comfortable space for everyone to get through the space or hang out without feeling cramped and being on top of one another.

In my own living room, flanking a pair of identical sofas around a coffee table made the most sense for the room.

Symmetrical furniture placement lends a sense of balance to this client's living room.

One of my favorite layouts for living rooms, and one that I have in my own house, is to have to identical sofas flanking the room, a great coffee table in the center with a minimum of fifteen inches of clearance all around it, and a fabulous pair of armchairs opposite a focal point. I use this arrangement in my work often because it feels very balanced, anchors a room quite nicely, provides plenty of seating, and works in just about any living room you can imagine. It's important to create special "moments" or vignettes in a space, so don't forget about walls and corners. The combination of a console table with great art, chic lamps, and ottomans or stools underneath for additional seating is not only stylish, but also adds functionality. Pedestals and floor lamps are also great for punctuating a room.

Having a couple of distinct, well-defined seating areas makes this very large room feel more intimate.

A Few Good Rules of Thumb:

• The ideal distance between the cocktail table and sofa is about 18".

• The best distance between two lounge chairs side-by-side is 42".

• You'll want to make sure that the rug in your space is as large as the room can handle. Nothing is worse than a postage stamp for a rug! Make sure that at least two of the legs on each piece of furniture are on the rug, but optimally, every piece will sit completely on top of the rug. The exception is in the dining room, where all of the legs must be on top of the rug with at least 3" beyond the edge of the dining table.

• The ideal distance between the edge of the rug and the wall is 12" to 24". Oftentimes, custom-cut seagrass rugs leave less distance between the rug and wall.

• Remember to keep a comfortable distance between your sofa and TV. It should be neither too close nor too far. The ideal distance is 1.5 times the size of your television.

• Don't push all of the furniture up against the walls! Your living room should feel warm and be conducive to conversation. It's not a middle school dance! Make sure to "float" at least one substantial piece in the room.

The expansive footprint
and two-story windows in
this living room called
for larger scale furniture.

SCALING UP

Scale is one of the most important elements of design. Small pieces of furniture and art can dwarf a small room even further, while large, cavernous spaces require large-scale pieces to fill the negative space. There is a fine line between "scaling up" or selecting a larger piece for visual impact and cramming in a piece of furniture that is just too big for the space! Scaled floor plans are super helpful in ensuring that everything is the ideal size for a room. They are a very important tool in our office because they help us to ensure that everything in my design will fit the way that it should and provide the client with peace of mind and a better ability to visualize how things will come together. If you still have doubts or seek a more hands-on approach, buy a roll of blue painter's tape and mark everything out in the room to ensure that everything fits and that there is a comfortable flow.

One of the first big projects I worked on after starting my firm was a very large, fairly new house. It had very high ceilings in most of the rooms and the people who owned the house before my client bought it had filled it with furniture that was much too small. As a result, each room looked cold and cavernous. I knew we could do better! By bringing in larger pieces, the spaces instantly felt much cozier and more welcoming. We were able to achieve visual balance and harmony, which leads to spaces that feel as good as they look.

Create a focal point and an unexpected element of surprise by having at least one great, large-scale piece in a room, whether it's a large painting, a huge mirror, or a substantially sized table lamp. These pieces add interest to the room and help to achieve balance.

(Left) A seagrass rug lends texture and a casual feel to this living room. *(Opposite)* A custom Moroccan wool rug adds a graphic touch to this modern dining room.

RUGS

While we are on the topic of scale, rugs can be tricky sometimes. One of the most common decorating mistakes is using a rug that is too small for the room. Nothing is worse than a living room with a tiny postage stamp of a rug that barely extends beyond the coffee table! Always go for the largest rug that a room can comfortably accommodate. The purpose of a rug from a design perspective is to add texture and to "ground" the room. Because rugs literally set the foundation of a room, they play an important role in the overall design scheme of a space and can act as the foundation for the overall color palette and textiles used.

While I love tailored, glamorous elements in design, I often use natural fiber rugs, which lend an effortless, relaxed quality to any room and usually keep it from feeling too formal. The other great thing about natural fiber rugs such as sea grass and sisal is that they are durable, neutral, and generally inexpensive. One of my favorite things to do, particularly in larger rooms that require a big rug, is to have a custom-cut seagrass rug made and then layer a casual, wool dhurrie with a great pattern on top of it.

In bedrooms, I usually opt for softer rugs that feel nice underfoot. Wool or wool-blend rugs are great options and are also a good way to inject color or pattern into a room. When using a modern, patterned rug, I generally go with stripes or a small-scale pattern that won't feel tired after a while. For rooms that call for a more classic rug, pale, vintage oushaks from Turkey are a beautiful and timeless option.

"In bedrooms,
I usually opt
for softer rugs
that feel nice
underfoot."

A custom geometric
wool rug adds
warmth and pattern
to this bedroom.

A custom-cut
seagrass rug
adds texture and
grounds this
client's otherwise
glamorous library.

Complementary pillow
fabrics include a
patterned anchor fabric
and a solid fabric to
tie the palette together.

FABRIC

Early on in the process of working on a new design project, I will select an anchor fabric. The anchor fabric is the star among the textiles in the room. It might be a solid color that ties everything together or a patterned fabric that serves as the statement in the room. Think of the anchor fabric as the hero in your textile scheme. Once I figure out the anchor fabric, I can make the selections for complementary fabrics, trims, rugs, and window treatments. I typically use solid fabrics on larger pieces of furniture and reserve patterned fabrics for things like pillows, window treatments, and the occasional chair, so my anchor fabric will usually be limited to one of these pieces, but because it is so fabulous, a little goes a long way. Every now and again, a really daring client who loves a lot of pattern will come along and we will have fun with vibrant prints, embroideries, and colors, but even then, the anchor fabric is normally the impetus for the overall vision.

The anchor fabric is typically a fabric that I am very inspired by and whose colors and pattern serve as a springboard for the rest of the room. I'll draw from the colors in the anchor fabric's pattern when selecting the rest of the fabrics for the room's design scheme. Because I live in Texas and most of my projects are located here, I often use linen fabrics, which are lightweight, cool, and breathable on upholstered pieces of furniture and almost always on window treatments. Small doses of velvet and silk on chairs or pillows add a bit of effortless glamour, while the occasional leather can imbue a masculine or modern air.

CHIC COMBINATIONS: *fabrics*

ANCHOR
FABRIC

SOLID

COORDINATING
PRINT

CLASSIC
GLAMOUR

MODERN
TRADITIONAL

ECLECTIC
COOL

CASUAL
CHIC

"Window treatments are functional…but they also serve the very important aesthetic purpose of framing the room."

WINDOW TREATMENTS

Window treatments are so important when it comes to having a room that truly feels finished. You can have a room filled with beautiful furniture and art, but if the windows are bare, it will look incomplete. Window treatments are functional, providing privacy and light filtration, but they also serve the very important aesthetic purpose of framing the room, much in the same way that a rug grounds it. There are rare occasions when windows don't require window coverings. For instance, with very modern architecture, a beautifully framed window, or a stunning view, you certainly wouldn't want any sort of obstruction. In general, however, most rooms will benefit from some kind of window treatment.

I always advise clients that window treatments are a high-ticket item once you factor in labor, all of that fabric yardage, trim, and hardware. For this reason, choose a classic combination of fabric and trim that you will not tire of anytime soon and could potentially move with you to your next house or stay in the room in the event that you decide to redesign it. The second, more daring, option is to embrace your anchor fabric and really commit to it by using it on your window treatment. If you love it enough, it will feel timeless and you will continue to love it for years.

Classic ivory linen curtains paired with grass shades add to the airy quality of this living room.

Classic linen drapery panels and simple hardware add softness to each of these rooms.

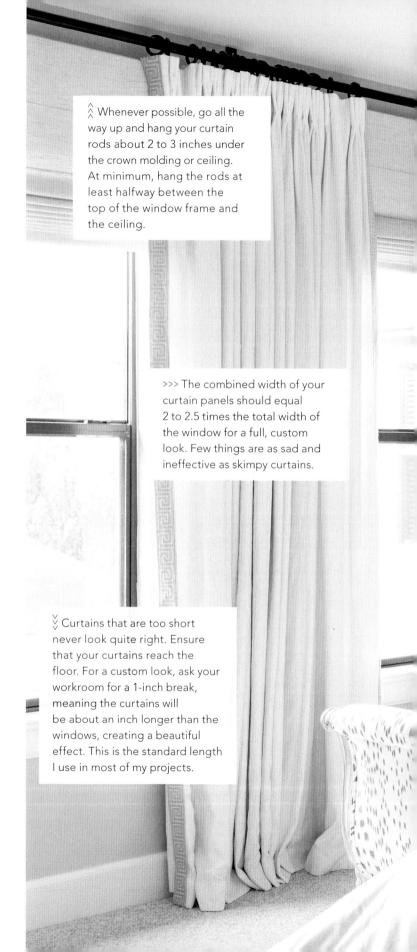

These simple guidelines will help you get your drapery treatments right every time.

^^ Whenever possible, go all the way up and hang your curtain rods about 2 to 3 inches under the crown molding or ceiling. At minimum, hang the rods at least halfway between the top of the window frame and the ceiling.

>>> The combined width of your curtain panels should equal 2 to 2.5 times the total width of the window for a full, custom look. Few things are as sad and ineffective as skimpy curtains.

v Curtains that are too short never look quite right. Ensure that your curtains reach the floor. For a custom look, ask your workroom for a 1-inch break, meaning the curtains will be about an inch longer than the windows, creating a beautiful effect. This is the standard length I use in most of my projects.

curtains

Curtains come in an endless array of styles, from casual iterations to very ornate ones worthy of haute couture. My go-to curtain style is a tailored linen curtain with a beautiful trim on the leading edge, a French pinch-pleat header, generous width, and a one-inch break on the length, which means that the bottom just touches the floor without any puddling. I always hang my curtains on rings and will either choose simple bronze or iron return rods that wrap around or a statement rod such as a Lucite one with beautiful aged brass hardware.

Calculating curtain lengths and widths is not for the faint of heart, so be sure to rely on your workroom if you are going the custom route. As a rule of thumb, there are a few common mistakes to avoid with curtains, so if you are opting for ready-made curtains you'll want to remember this advice.

<<< It is just as important for the curtains to be the right length as it is for the curtain rods to be the correct width. Depending on the size of your windows, rods should ideally extend 6 to 12 inches beyond the window frame. Doing so gives the windows a fuller look and ensures that the bulk of your curtains will sit on the outer part of the window rather than covering the window and blocking natural light.

A variety of Roman shade styles in a few clients' homes as well as in my living room.

roman shades

Roman shades are a great option in more casual settings as well as in areas where the privacy and texture offered by window treatments are desired, but the length of traditional curtains is not an option. Roman shades come in a variety of styles: flat, relaxed, hobbled, balloon, and so on. My favorite style for fabric shades is a flat roman with a complementary tape trim. The addition of the trim makes it feel a little more polished and special, but the flat style still feels effortless and lies really nicely on the window.

Roman shades also come in a variety of natural weaves, which look great on their own in a more casual space or when paired with curtains for additional privacy and a contrasting texture.

Pay special attention to the way that roman shades are hung. They can be hung two ways—inside mount or outside mount. If you have beautiful millwork or are constricted by space outside of the window frame, usually due to cabinetry, you should opt for an inside-mount frame. Otherwise, choose an outside mount that will give the illusion of a larger window and make the shade itself feel fuller.

When pairing roman shades with curtains, hang your shades at the same height as the curtain rod, above the window frame, in order to eliminate unsightly negative space. The result draws the eye up, creating the optical illusion of larger windows and a more open space.

LIGHTING

Lighting is my very favorite element of design. It truly is the jewelry of any space. Lighting has the important task of both adding to the aesthetic beauty of a room and also setting the mood by imparting the proper type and amount of light. Lighting is divided into two major types: decorative and ambient lighting. It is then further divided into several categories: table, floor, ceiling, and wall. As a general rule of thumb, lamplight is the most flattering, casting a warm glow over a room without the harshness of overhead light. Chandeliers and sconces are ideal for filling a room with light and punctuating architectural features. Recessed cans are typically used in addition to decorative lighting. I prefer to limit them to kitchens, bathrooms, and hallways where they deliver the necessary amount of light. Try not to go overboard with too many recessed cans because they are often unnecessary and can look unattractive. That being said, if you have recessed can lights in your house, do not worry! You can easily correct what are commonly thought of as their negative effects by installing a dimmer switch and changing to a more flattering type of light bulb.

A tall, gilded,
plaster chandelier is
the perfect scale
for the high ceilings in
this breakfast room.

When planning the lighting for a room, it is helpful to think about the various sources of light and how you would use them. For example, in my own kitchen we have three sources of light in addition to the natural light from the window. We have recessed cans for general ambient lighting, decorative pendants over the island and the sink, and LED under-cabinet lights for additional task and ambient lighting during food prep. Each of these sources is on its own switch, which means that we can manipulate the light to set the mood we need in any given situation. For instance, if we have friends coming over drinks, we will turn on the pendants and under-cabinet lighting for a soft, inviting glow. If we're busy preparing a meal, we prefer to have the recessed cans and under-cabinet lights on for maximum light.

When it comes to lamplight, choosing the right light bulb is very important. LED light bulbs have come a long way and are not only energy efficient, but can look great when you choose the right type. I prefer soft white for the warm glow of incandescent bulbs. Also, remember to choose a lower wattage than the maximum your lamp calls for. For instance, if your table lamp calls for a 100 watt maximum bulb, use a 40 watt bulb so that it gives off soft, flattering light. After all, the purpose of decorative or ambient lamps is to reveal the mood of the space. On the other hand, task lights are used for reading or illuminating art or architectural features. Once you've determined the specifics of the type of lighting your room needs, the real fun can begin! Lighting is a great way to make a statement and imbue your environment with your desired style. Do you want your room to feel glamorous and feminine or masculine and modern? Lighting is the perfect way to set the mood and style of the space.

CHIC COMBINATIONS: *lighting*

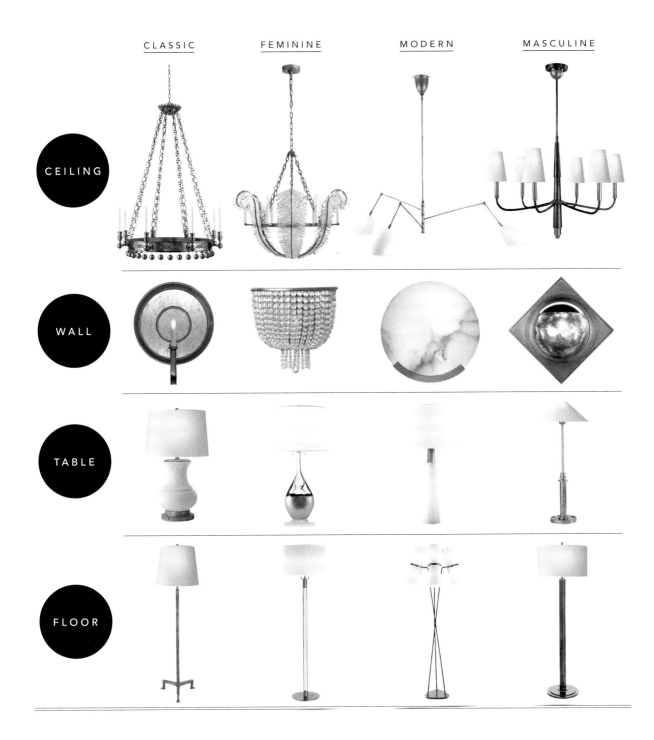

	CLASSIC	FEMININE	MODERN	MASCULINE
CEILING				
WALL				
TABLE				
FLOOR				

Louis XVI Chairs

Bamboo Details

blue & White pottery

Chinoiserie Wallpaper

potted orchid

black & white abstract art

Saarinen Tulip Table

skirted sofa
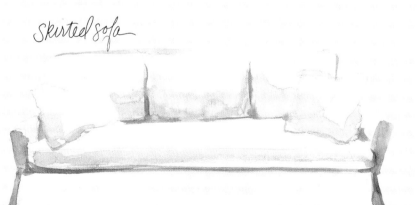

Potted Myrtle Topiaries

Sconce

A few of my favorite things: black-and-white abstract art, a parsons table, blue-and-white accents, and chic brass lamps. (Illustrations by Inslee Fariss)

Convex Mirror

Ikat Fabrics

FOREVER CLASSICS

Some things are just so good—so beautifully designed and versatile—that they never go out of style and are universally loved. There are some timeless, workhorse pieces that can work in just about any environment, adding a dose of good taste and chic style regardless of what they are paired with. Just about all of these pieces have become indispensable elements that I use in nearly every design project for their great lines, versatility, and effortless style.

BEAUTIFUL BEDROOMS

Our bedrooms are not only where we begin each day and get energized to face the world each morning, but they are also where we go to rest and recharge each evening. Can you think of a space that serves a more important function than setting the tone for the type of day we might have? Because of this, I am a firm believer that bedrooms should be beautiful. While it is fun to embrace color and take risks in children's rooms and guest bedrooms, I usually find it best to design master bedrooms that are soothing and have a sense of harmony.

There is no need to overthink bedroom designs. While other spaces in the house might get a little trickier in terms of furniture placement, bedrooms are usually very straightforward. Opt for a bed with a classic silhouette, be it upholstered or wood—this is usually an investment piece, so be sure it is something you would want to live with for years to come. Please avoid the "furniture-store look" and

I always start with crisp, white bedding, then layer in color and pattern.

Details like custom lampshades and monogrammed linens can make any bedroom feel special.

avoid buying a matching bed and nightstands at all costs! The look is boring and has no personality. While the pieces should complement one another, there should be some contrast to keep things interesting. I am a big proponent of symmetry and the bedroom is no exception. I prefer matching nightstands over different ones because I find them more pleasing to the eye. Nightstands with concealed storage, whether in the form of drawers or doors, are my preference because they keep things like novels, iPads, cell phones, remotes, reading glasses, and other knick knacks concealed. On each nightstand, add a nice lamp, preferably one with a couple of settings in case you prefer to read with a lower level of light in the evenings. It's nice to punctuate the area near the bed with either a piece of art or a mirror over the headboard or above each nightstand. Bedside tables are the perfect canvas for framed photographs and personal mementos since these rooms are more private than other rooms in the house.

This client's bedroom *(left)* has a serene effect thanks to a calming color palette.

Invest in the best linens and mattress that you can afford because a great night's sleep has a huge effect on your health and happiness! It's always good to have plenty of seating in a space, even in bedrooms. I like to create a separate seating area with a pair of chairs or a single cozy lounge chair, a matching ottoman, a great little drinks table, and a floor lamp. This setup is perfect for reading and relaxing. If you have the space, it is always nice to add a pretty upholstered bench or a pair of ottomans at the foot of the bed. Not only does it give you a place to sit while putting on or taking off your shoes, it also helps to punctuate and define the room.

Sweet, feminine details
include a scalloped
chair skirt and pink tape
trim on the curtains.

children's bedrooms

I love designing spaces for children because they tend to be colorful and more whimsical than other rooms in the house. I also approach them with the goal of creating a beautiful, vibrant, and nurturing environment that feels age appropriate. Sometimes my clients might argue that keeping children's rooms neat and orderly can be an uphill battle and that it is hard to win the case for design when a child is hell-bent on a room with a "theme" based on a character from their favorite movie. I have found that it helps to give the children a voice and allow them to feel involved in the process, even if it is in a small way, such as helping to pick the paint color for the walls. With some positive affirmation and guidance, the process always yields wonderful results. For instance, I once had a client whose eight-year-old son was obsessed with sports, so much so that he had a giant, life-size decal of his favorite football player plastered on his wall. His mother is very design savvy, so while she led the charge in determining the direction she wanted me to take for his bedroom, we made sure to speak to him about what was important to him and what his prized possessions were.

A dramatic custom canopy in a rose chintz by Dorothy Draper for Schumacher is the focal point of this little girl's room.

This young boy's
room features David
Hicks's La Fiorentina
fabric and Farrow &
Ball's rich and moody
Hague Blue paint.

We ended up painting the room Farrow & Ball's Hague Blue and incorporated
David Hicks's La Fiorentina fabric into several elements of the room, including
the window coverings, a custom chair, and a large bolster pillow for the bed.
We had custom built-ins made to allow him to display his signed baseballs and
footballs and his Lego creations. The little boy was thrilled because his new
room was painted in a variation of his favorite color and he had plenty of space
to show off his favorite things. His mother was happy because the room felt
polished, had plenty of storage to keep toys organized and concealed, and was
designed to be the type of room that her son can grow into.

(Below) A cohesive color palette extends across various elements in this teen's room. (Opposite) Cole & Son's Hummingbirds wallpaper creates a dreamy backdrop in this nursery.

CHAPTER FOUR

FORM AND FUNCTION

According to the popular adage, the kitchen is the heart of the home. So much happens in the kitchen, from food prep and casual meals around the breakfast table to homework and school projects crafted on the kitchen island. Kitchens have truly become the most multipurpose, hardest working rooms in most houses. I am a classicist at my core and tend to skew a tad more conservative and traditional in the kitchens I design for my clients. I have yet to tire of beautiful white kitchens. In my mind, few things are as classic or enduring. As I have mentioned before, I tend to be averse to trends, so of course, I would caution you against executing any major, of-the-moment trends in your kitchen, because it could result in an expensive design decision that you'll come to tire of sooner than you had initially anticipated. My high school French teacher's 1970s canary yellow kitchen comes to mind. Everything was yellow, from the laminate countertops to the cabinet hardware and the appliances. I'm sure it must have had a blip on the radar of fabulousness, but by the late 1990s when I visited her house for a French club event, it felt tired and dated. Rather than repeat this mistake of embracing a current trend on every surface of a room, when it comes to kitchen and bath design, I tend to embrace a classic color palette, timeless design elements, and durable surfaces. These spaces should be functional, inviting, and beautiful and you can easily achieve all three of these goals.

(This page and following spread)
A classic color palette, distinctive fixtures, and a custom range hood make this kitchen classic.

CHIC COMBINATIONS: *the kitchen*

CABINET COLOR	COUNTERTOP	FAUCET	CABINET HARDWARE	LIGHTING

CLASSIC GLAMOUR

MODERN TRADITIONAL

ECLECTIC COOL

CASUAL CHIC

Light gray cabinets, a statuary marble slab backsplash and countertops, and antique mirror insets create a seamless, enduring look in this modern, yet timeless kitchen.

"A beautifully designed room can feel both modern and classic through the thoughtful use of materials and the creation of an overall look that has a timeless quality."

Traditional definitely doesn't have to mean boring, and timeless and modern aren't mutually exclusive. A beautifully designed room can feel both modern and classic through the thoughtful use of materials and the creation of an overall look that has a timeless quality. The key is to start with a neutral palette and clean lines and then layer in interest. This can be achieved with special design details such as a beautiful range hood, mixing metal finishes, selecting a rich paint color for the cabinetry, and adding statement-making lighting and cabinet hardware, which act as the jewelry of the kitchen.

Kitchens are expensive to renovate. They always cost more than you would imagine, which is why I am a huge advocate of embracing timeless materials and classic finishes in kitchens. You'll get so much more mileage out of your kitchen this way! Thankfully, if your kitchen is in good shape you can make drastic improvements through cosmetic updates.

Our kitchen update has been one of my favorite transformations in our house. While we didn't do a major renovation, the changes we made were quite impactful. Our kitchen is a wonderful example of how the right finishes can completely elevate a space when you have good bones to work with. One of the things that really sold us on our house was the quality and craftsmanship of the millwork. We have beautiful moldings and everything is really solid. When we first saw the

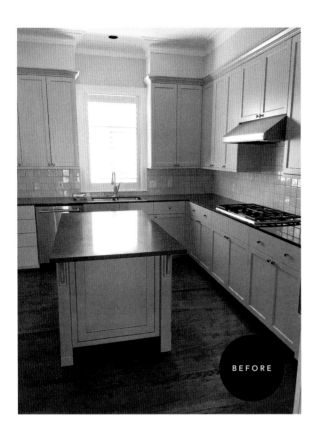

BEFORE

I gave my kitchen a face-lift by keeping the things that worked—the cabinets and layout—and updating those that didn't, like the dingy backsplash, dated faucet and cabinet hardware, and old appliances.

house, I liked the soft greige hue of the cabinets as well as the fact that they are inset and have simple, Shaker-style doors, which are very timeless. I also knew instantly that I did not love the other selections or the color palette in the kitchen's previous iteration. Because of the footprint of the space, there wasn't a need to make any structural changes. The kitchen's existing layout has a pretty good flow and is the best use of the space, so we set out to make cosmetic improvements.

I knew right away that I wanted to get rid of the old backsplash in the kitchen when we bought the house. While it had a nice handmade quality to it, the yellow undertones in the beige tile looked dingy to me and really didn't work with the color of the cabinets. The granite countertops looked nearly black when looking at them from a distance, but were actually more of a dark green, which dated the house to 2001, when it was built. To update the hard surfaces, I opted for classic, budget-friendly subway tile. I used it in my last house and loved it so much that I decided to go with it again. I absolutely love the look of marble in a kitchen, but am also very much aware that my personality would make living with marble in the kitchen challenging for me. Fabian and I love to cook and we also enjoy our fair share of wine, so etching and staining would be inevitable and I would likely fixate on stains. Instead, we opted for a white quartz countertop with gray veining, which works very nicely with the backsplash and cabinet color.

"To add a bit of glamour and contrast, I infused a bit of gold into the space through the light fixtures I selected. If you have ever wondered if it is okay to mix metal finishes, the answer is a resounding yes!"

Mixing metal finishes on design elements like cabinet hardware and plumbing fixtures can make a kitchen feel more layered and interesting.

The simple cabinet hardware previously in our kitchen was fine, but I knew that I would want to switch from commonly used brushed nickel to my favorite metal finish, polished nickel. As much as I love brass and feel that aged brass is certainly a classic, the fact that brass has been a huge trend over the past several years cemented my decision to use timeless polished nickel for the cabinet hardware and plumbing fixtures instead. To add a bit of glamour and contrast, I infused a bit of gold into the space through the light fixtures I selected. If you have ever wondered if it is okay to mix metal finishes, the answer is a resounding yes! I frequently mix metals in just about every room that I design. A mix of metals gives space warmth, depth of character, and a hint of glamour. You have to edit carefully, though. My suggestion is to select almost everything in one finish and use a different finish on either the cabinet hardware or lighting in order to achieve a seamless look. A good general rule of thumb is to use the same finish on the plumbing fixtures and cabinet hardware, but it is okay to use a different finish on the lighting and door hardware. Just as in any other room in the house, there has to be a common thread that ties everything together and creates a sense of harmony and cohesion in the space.

A crisp, white color palette with graceful sconces, faucets, and a custom Roman shade with a pretty tape trim in this marble-clad bathroom ensures that my clients will love this space for many years.

BATHING BEAUTIES

Like kitchens, bathrooms are among the most utilized spaces in a house and as such, they should be highly functional. However, that does not mean that they shouldn't also be beautiful. The style of the bathrooms in a home should be in keeping with the overall look and feel of the rest of the house so that everything feels cohesive. For instance, if you have a very traditional house, a super modern bathroom with a floating vanity, minimal mirror, and contemporary fixtures is jarring and out of place. That being said, if you choose classic materials overall, you can certainly mix in some modern elements like cool sconces or more streamlined faucets. The key is to create a layered look rather than a completely alien concept. My philosophy about eschewing trends and relegating of-the-moment design elements to other spaces holds especially true in both kitchens and bathrooms since they are generally the most expensive rooms to renovate. Translation: you'll most likely have to live with your design decisions for a very long time!

Glamorous new sconces, gleaming new hardware, and soft taupe paint transformed my master bathroom into an elegant oasis.

The master bathroom was the very last thing we finished in our new house. I had wanted to do it before we moved in, but we did not have enough time between our closing date and the end of the lease-back on our old house. If you can manage to renovate your kitchen and bathrooms without living in your house, do it! I had to live through the less-than-ideal scenario of unpacking and trying to settle into a new house while the demolition and renovation of the bathroom took place. Ripping out tile creates more dust than you could ever imagine! It ends up in places that it has no business being in. It was so loud and our dog, Tate, who goes crazy when we have workers in the house, had to go stay with my mother-in-law for much longer than I would have liked. The previous owners of our house had put in new Carrara marble floors and counter-tops, along with new lavatory faucets, but everything else was in original condition.

My client and I wanted to
do something really special
in her master bathroom.
In order to create a "WOW"
moment, we tiled a huge wall
with a hexagonal mosaic
tile that became the focal point
of the bathroom.

While the Carrara was a nice addition, the ceramic subway tile in the shower and around the tub was about three shades too warm for the marble, so I replaced it. The old flooring was large format, twenty-inch squares of Carrara marble tile. Paired with the countertops, it felt like there was too much "movement" in the space due to all of the veining in the marble. We decided to work with the existing countertops, so to soften the overall look, we opted for a hexagonal mosaic in Carrara marble. In order to keep things classic and clean, we used subway tile in the shower, but went for a Carrara marble version to make the space feel more luxurious. We finished off the space with gleaming new plumbing fixtures, sconces, and mirrors, all in polished nickel.

What was once a terribly dated 1980s bathroom received a major overhaul using more current and classic selections.

When it comes to master bathrooms, stick with enduring elements, add a statement through beautiful lighting, plumbing fixtures, and tile, and most importantly, keep it classic. Once you've decided on the overall look, color palette, and materials you would like to work with, you'll want to consider the elements that will make using your bathroom as enjoyable as possible. If you live in a colder climate, radiant-heat flooring can be an amazing luxury in the winters, while migraine or sinus-headache sufferers might find the addition of a steam shower to be a lifesaver. Custom vanities with drawer organizers and hidden electrical outlets are not only modern-day conveniences that increase functionality, but also a way to keep things neat and looking lovely. Ultimately, your bathroom is where you go to get ready for the day ahead, and in the evening, where you go to recharge and unwind, so why not make the space a little indulgent rather than purely utilitarian? More and more, people are incorporating luxury amenities such as sculptural freestanding tubs and coffee bars into their bathrooms. Not everyone needs all of the bells and whistles, but you should tailor your bathroom to your personal preferences. If you enjoy a leisurely, nightly bath, it might make sense to splurge on the best tub on the market. If you find showers most invigorating, you may opt for multiple sprays and showerheads.

In my own powder room, I opted for a graphic grisaille wallpaper, Cole & Son's Fornasetti Nuvolette Cloud.

GO FOR THE BOLD

Children's bathrooms and powder bathrooms are among my favorite spaces to design because they bring about the opportunity to have fun and make a bold statement. Because these spaces tend to be smaller than a master bathroom, the same rules do not necessarily apply. Small spaces provide the opportunity to make a statement and be a bit more daring than usual. Powder rooms are completely contained unto themselves, so if there is statement wallpaper, a bold paint color or application, or a special detail such as trelliswork that you have been hoping to try, this is the place to do it!

When we moved into our new house, I was super excited to have a powder room because our first house had only had full bathrooms. It may seem like an odd thing to get excited about, but for me, a powder bath meant one thing—wallpaper! I have loved Fornasetti's Nuvolette wallpaper, available through Cole and Son, for ages. It is a black-and-white pattern composed of dreamy clouds and I had been dying to use it for quite a while. Because large-scale patterns can feel overwhelming in big spaces, I knew that my powder room would be the perfect place for it. The wallpaper truly envelops the space and creates a "wow" moment in my house. Even the most conservative, risk-averse clients will come to me asking for wallpaper in their powder rooms since it is a great way to infuse a small space with a huge dose of style and to express your personality.

WALLPAPER	VANITY	FAUCET	MIRRORS	LIGHTING
CLASSIC GLAMOUR				
MODERN TRADITIONAL				
ECLECTIC COOL				
CASUAL CHIC				

A Few Good Rules of Thumb

• Before starting a bathroom or kitchen remodel, consult with a professional contractor. DIY television shows have fooled countless people into thinking that such renovations are a breeze! You'll want to consult with a professional in these two rooms more than any other because mistakes can be incredibly costly and you will end up spending more in the end without someone who understands design and construction standards, codes, and regulations.

• While most people opt for chrome for kitchen and bathroom hardware and plumbing fixtures because it is neutral and easy to clean, I prefer polished nickel for its warm undertones and elegant finish. It works beautifully with both cool and warm colors, unlike chrome, which reads very blue.

• I love the look of aged brass, but it is best used sparingly when it comes to plumbing fixtures. Put it in a room where it can really make a statement, such as your powder room, and stick with polished nickel in the kitchen and master bathroom.

• Lighting is a great way to introduce a new finish to a space and mix metals. It looks super chic to have polished nickel or bronze cabinet hardware and plumbing fixtures with brass lighting or vice versa. Mixing metals adds a layer of richness and personality to a space!

• Remember to keep your storage needs in mind as you plan the design of your bathroom. You will want to have plenty of room to keep everything hidden away so that your bathroom is organized and tidy.

• Plan to have 36" to 40" between vanity sconces for optimum light dispersion.

• Towel bars should be hung 48" from the ground while robe hooks should be hung at a height of 60" above the ground.

• When selecting materials, think about how much maintenance you are comfortable with and whether it is worth it to you in order to use a beautiful material you love.

• If your budget won't allow for you to completely renovate your bathroom, you can still give it a major facelift with freshly painted walls and cabinetry, new plumbing fixtures, lighting, and linens.

• Don't forget to decorate your bathroom! A few personal touches like art, a pretty rug, and baskets for storage add texture, interest, color, and personality to one of the most utilitarian spaces in the house.

Everything has its place in our office. Custom built-in desks and storage towers ensure that we have plenty of space and that the studio is always neat and orderly.

STYLISH WORKSPACES

Our surroundings can have a major impact on our state of mind, so having a stylish, organized workspace—whether it is a home office, a traditional study, or a library—can be paramount in one's level of productivity. In my own office, I prioritize plenty of concealed storage, so that everything is in its place at all times. When we redesigned and built out our office, I knew that I wanted to add custom cabinetry so that all of our baskets of fabric samples, finish samples, client binders, and vendor catalogs could be concealed behind doors. Messes make me a little crazy, so not having to look at so many design elements brings me a sense of peace and allows me to focus on designing new spaces for my clients.

A calming paint color can set the tone for a work space that enables creativity and encourages organization. This lacquered blue-gray hue is ideal.

Since we generally work on a dozen different design projects at any given moment, it was also important for the design of our office to be neutral since the color palette and fabric selections can vary greatly from one project to the next. I did not want our office environment to compete or interfere with our design work and creativity, so our cabinetry is white with custom-made pulls in Lucite and antique brass; we have a chic pendant hanging above our tulip work table with marble top; the girls on my team have white task lamps with brass accents; and we have leopard carpet, which is the wild card in the space. The obvious choice may have been seagrass, but my dog, Tate, spends the entire day in the office with us, so it was important for the carpet to be soft enough for him and for the rest of us when we work on presentation boards and other projects on the floor. After all, leopard is a neutral!

Even the smallest
work space can
be efficient if you have
plenty of storage, a
comfortable chair, and
good lighting.

Whether your workspace is a separate office or a little nook with a desk somewhere in your house, there are a few things to keep in mind. You'll need a desk and a comfortable chair, along with good overhead and task lighting in the form of a desk lamp. Remember to factor in enough storage for your needs, particularly if you are converting a bedroom into an office space. On the other hand, you may opt to put a small desk with a chair and lamp in a dedicated library, but if the space is mainly used for relaxing with a good book, you will want to ensure that you have plenty of cozy seating and lighting in the form of table or floor lamps to help set the mood. Again, plenty of shelving and storage is very important, so be sure to assess your space. You may be surprised—not only by how much shelving or cabinetry you can add, but also by the amazing way that it can transform a space.

In my living room, graphic abstract art and fabrics add contrast and visual interest.

CHAPTER FIVE

IT'S ALL IN THE DETAILS

If a floor plan, rugs, furniture, and lighting create the foundation of a room, the details are what truly bring it to life. Items such as accessories, art, and books tell more about your personality, taste, and individual story than a sofa or dining table ever could. In addition to adding layers of style, interest, and your personal story to a space, decorative accessories and objects can also be used to create focal points and train the eye to go to the places in the room that you would like to emphasize or amplify. Envision a living room with a couple of beautiful custom sofas, some chic lamps on end tables, a statement-making coffee table, a rug, and some draperies. The room might be filled with stylish elements, but it would look and feel incomplete. It isn't until you layer in art, add a fabulous mix of throw pillows to the sofa, stack some interesting books and objects to the coffee table, and add fresh flowers that a room truly feels pulled together. Just imagine flipping through your favorite magazine and seeing a house that did not include these elements. It would never happen because such a house would feel lifeless!

SLIM AARONS · LA DOLCE VITA

THE NEW SHINGLED HOUSE   IKE KLIGERMAN BARKLEY

JAM
HAMPT

MERICAN BEAUTY   ASSOULINE

DERIAN

Accessories are the final layer of a space. They punctuate the design and help to tie the details together.

When designing our clients' homes, we often work accessories and art into the overall design plan, but more often than not, we have a separate styling process at the end, usually during the installation, during which we bring in accessories, art, interesting objects, and flowers to complete the space and give it the layered look and feeling that our clients crave when they come to us. Adding decorative accessories also helps to amplify the mood of the room, which could be playful, casual, formal, and so on. Objects such as accessories, art, books, and personal mementos work together to create a visual narrative about your home, and more importantly, about you! While it is important to add pieces that infuse the space with personality, it is just as imperative to be a fierce editor. Clutter is the enemy, while cleverly arranged vignettes and great styling can completely transform a room.

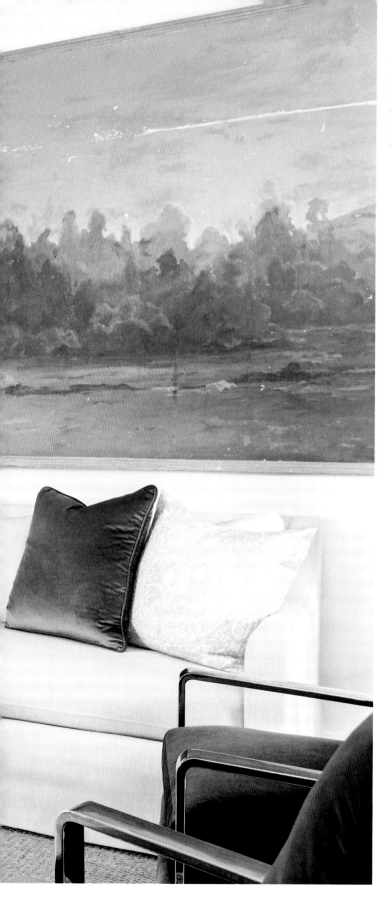

My client inherited this beautiful antique landscape painting from her parents. It is the focal point of the room and inspired the entire color palette.

ART

Art is so incredibly personal that I find it to be one of the most difficult things to source, especially for clients. At the very least, art is decorative. It should either work seamlessly with the space it is in, or conversely, it can serve as a striking counterpoint that shakes things up, such as a modern abstract painting in an otherwise very traditional room. In addition, art is evocative. In most cases, unless the homeowner is completely indifferent to art, it has to make the viewer feel something and play into setting the mood of the space. The bottom line is, you have to love it and it has to make you feel good when you look at it. That can happen for a variety of reasons. If you are lucky, your artwork could be a significant, blue-chip piece that is a big coup for you. For most of us, it simply means that the piece strikes a chord—possibly because it is by a favorite artist or because it evokes a special memory.

(Left) A large scale black-and-white abstract painting punctuates my stairwell. *(Opposite)* An indigo abstract painting by William McLure adds a bold dose of color to this client's living room.

Good art does not have to be prohibitive so long as you are creative and resourceful. Many up-and-coming artists sell directly to their followers online, sometimes selling small pieces of original art for a song! Thrift shops, antiques stores, and antiques shows such as Round Top and Brimfield are also wonderful sources for finding and procuring affordable, original art. In some cases, you may like the frame more than the art itself, so you can repurpose it. If you are so inclined, you can also paint pieces yourself. In our first house, I painted several abstract pieces myself and also printed and framed black-and-white photos taken by my husband on our travels, some of which I still have on display in our new house. These pieces may not be expensive or valuable to anyone else, but they help to tell our story. If your budget does not have room for investment art, then textiles, maps, and even nice wrapping paper can make a statement if you put them in nice enough frames. There are also great websites such as Artfully Walls, One Kings Lane, and Saatchi Art, which sell limited edition and reproduction prints that will give you a lot of style for the price. It is totally fine to have a mix of original and reproduction pieces in your house. I won't tell!

This client is passionate about art and has amassed a very special collection over the years that acts as the centerpiece of the design of her home.

(Opposite) Sometimes a single piece of art, such as the striped ribbon painting by Angela Chrusciaki Blehm in my stairwell landing, can carry an entire space. (Below) Meanwhile, in my living room, I chose to surround my TV with art by Kayce Hughes, Alexis Walter, Anna Ullman, and others in order to disguise it a bit and to add some interest to that wall.

Once you have culled your artwork, you will have to go through the exercise of hanging it. When we first moved to our new house, I was thrilled by the more traditional layout the rooms have. After living in a new build with an open floor plan for ten years, I could not have been more excited to have walls everywhere! As a designer, I love walls. They lend structure and definition and also provide the opportunity to display art and mirrors. I have arranged things in various ways throughout the house. I begin by assessing the overall look of the room and how much art it can handle. A small space with lots of patterned fabrics is not the best place for a gallery or salon wall, for instance, as it would result in visual clutter and noise.

A single large statement piece can anchor a room or vignette. If a piece is large and special enough, you certainly will not want to detract from it and should let it stand on its own. Another look I love and that truly imparts a great deal of style to a room is a carefully planned grid. A grid tends to look best in tight groupings—at minimum four larger pieces or up to twelve smaller ones, usually hung two to three inches apart from one another so that they read as one bold statement. This works really nicely in spaces where the overall look is a bit softer and more feminine. Perhaps such a space would not be able to handle a large, bold painting, but a group of nine framed botanicals or antique intaglios is just as impactful visually without disrupting the serenity of the space.

A chic way to display art is to lean it on bookshelves or even on the floor. Something about this feels very European and has a bit of a carefree element, which is great for grounding an otherwise formal room to keep it from being over the top. Sometimes a grouping of art can serve to frame or disguise a feature you may not be crazy about. For instance, in my living room, I hung quite a few beautiful pieces of art in a mix of simple, modern frames and ornate gold leaf ones around my television so that the focal point of that wall wasn't solely a big, black rectangle. It makes me happy every time I see it.

ON THIS EARTH, A SHADOW FALLS   NICK BRAND

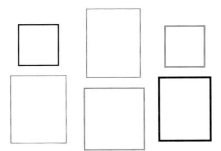

Very large walls like this one require more than one piece of art to feel complete.

HOW TO HANG A CHIC GALLERY WALL

When it comes to salon or gallery walls, it seems people either love them or hate them. I still like them, when used in the right setting. For instance, a long hallway can be a perfect opportunity to display a group of art or photography. The key to success is to have a solid plan in place before you start swinging a hammer.

1 Begin by deciding which pieces to group together. There should be unifying elements such as similar colors as well as a good mix of frames. If all of the frames are the same, the overall look will fall flat, but you want to ensure that there is a good balance. Try not to have more than two finishes on your frames to avoid visual chaos that will detract from the art itself.

2 Measure the wall where the art will be hung and then lay all of the pieces out in the desired arrangement on the floor, in an area of the same size as the wall where it will hang.

3 First, decide which piece will serve as the anchor in the center of the arrangement. It should hang at eye level, which is equal to about five and a half feet from the floor.

4 Next, on the floor, add other complementary pieces around the anchor piece. Things should be a little off-kilter and should not line up perfectly. If you want to be very precise, cut kraft paper templates to stand in for each piece of art.

5 It may take a few tries to get the placement exactly the way you want it. Once you do, take a photo of the arrangement. If you've created paper templates for each of the pieces, transfer them to the wall using painter's tape.

6 Hang the anchor piece (remove the paper template first) and check to ensure that it is level, then hang the other pieces around it.

(Opposite) In this living room, a pair of chunky seagrass baskets adds texture and storage for the children's toys. *(Right)* Boxes and trays in different shapes and finishes can look great when grouped together.

BASKETS, BOXES, AND TRAYS

Baskets, boxes, and trays provide a great way to keep a space organized. Baskets and boxes are good for keeping things like toys and remote controls contained and hidden, while trays are wonderful for displaying items in a way that feels neat and intentional. I love natural fiber baskets because they are neutral and are a great way to add texture to a space. There are many beautiful styles to choose from. Boxes are fantastic and somewhat underrated. You can group several small silver boxes together on a nightstand or end table for a sweet, traditional look. There are also stunning brass boxes with natural stone accents and bone-inlaid boxes that look amazing on a stack of books atop a coffee table or on a console. Trays are pretty ubiquitous and come in as many shapes, sizes, as finishes as you can imagine—rectangular, square, or round; lacquer, Lucite, metal, or woven, there is truly a tray for everyone. Trays can work in a million different settings, whether you are styling one with a couple of books, a decorative object, and a vase filled with flowers on your coffee table, or creating a makeshift bar on top of a console. All of these stylish storage options bring together form and function and are easy to integrate into any space seamlessly.

SMALL PIECE, BIG IMPACT

One of the unwritten rules of design is that rooms should feel intimate. An astute designer can make the most cavernous space feel cozy and inviting. Doing so takes an arsenal of tools, including the ever-important occasional table. Small tables and stools help to punctuate a space visually, but more importantly, they give your guests a place to set their drinks and can function as additional seating in a pinch. Coffee tables tend to be "styled" and as such, don't always leave a lot of room for practical things like drinks and remotes. A small occasional or "drinks" table, as I like to call it, not only provides a way to incorporate a great-looking piece into a room, but is also very practical when placed next to a sofa or between a pair of chairs.

Accent pieces, such as drink tables or small chests, can add big style.

Another great place for a small table or stool is next to a cozy lounge chair in a bedroom. I frequently create a reading nook in clients' bedrooms, which consists of a big, cozy chair, sometimes with an ottoman; a small occasional table or garden stool; and a floor lamp to create the perfect place to curl up with a book and a cup of tea—or glass of rosé, I'm not judging! The possibilities for these small pieces with a big impact are truly endless. For example, a console table always looks better with something underneath it, so consider a pair of ottomans or ceramic garden stools.

Metallic accents, fresh cut flowers "en masse," and graphic patterns add a glamorous touch to my living room.

A HINT OF GLAMOUR

Every room, no matter the style, needs a hint of glamour. It doesn't have to be something super obvious that slaps you across the face, because a little goes a long way. Even a rustic room can benefit from a touch of luxe. I have mentioned before that I enjoy mixing metals because it creates a more layered, interesting look. Decorative objects and accessories in metallic finishes are a great, easy way of adding a little bit of glamour to a room. Anything with even the slightest reflective quality can make a space feel more glamorous. Think brass, mercury glass, polished nickel, Lucite, antiqued mirror, or even bronze in anything from a vase or bowl to a picture frame or mirror. Remember, it's all about balance. A woven basket or decorative wooden box looks fabulous when juxtaposed against something a bit more glamorous. Design is all about creating the right amount of tension between different pieces.

HOW TO STYLE YOUR COFFEE TABLE

Coffee tables are a great canvas for displaying some of our favorite things. While they should feel layered, they shouldn't feel cluttered. Start by treating the coffee table as you would the room as a whole and set the foundation with larger items such as coffee table books and a large tray. When selecting coffee table books, limit your stacks to no more than three books each so that the coffee table doesn't look cluttered. I like to stack the books in different directions to create a more interesting look. Next, add a few objects such as decorative boxes, a candle, or a bowl of matchbooks on top of the books, making sure to create different levels. Lastly, layer in a natural element such as a potted orchid or plant or a pretty vase with fresh-cut flowers to complete the look.

Stacks of books, decorative boxes, bowls or trays, and fresh cut flowers are my must-haves for coffee-table styling.

In my living room, the built-in bookshelves display an assortment of my favorite books, small paintings, and a pair of plaster sunburst mirrors I bought in Paris.

STYLING BOOKSHELVES

Bookshelves can be tricky and they take a lot of trial and error. I have found that time and time again, clients will come to me feeling completely overwhelmed by what to do with their built-in bookcases and étagères. I will start by sharing what I feel is truly the most important thing to remember when it comes to styling bookshelves—you have to have *books*! I always find it slightly shocking when I come across pictures of a room with tons of bookshelves filled with random knick knacks and objects and nary a book in sight. The whole point of bookshelves is to store *books*, after all. Hopefully, you enjoy books as much as I do and have a healthy collection at home. If you don't, it's never too late to start collecting books on your travels and about various subjects that you are passionate about. If you're still not inclined to spend money on books, pretend! Go to the discount bookstore and buy books with nice-looking covers and spines to arrange among your tchotchkes.

Mixing decorative objects, vases, bowls, and framed art into your bookshelves is a great way to add color and character.

When starting to tackle the styling of a large set of bookcases, I begin by taking a visual inventory of everything I have to work with. This can include books, decorative accessories, potted topiaries, ginger jars, framed art and photographs, bowls, and boxes. Next, I choose larger books with neutral-colored spines and begin by adding them on the shelves at eye level.

The shelves at eye level serve as the anchor of the bookcase. I lay the foundation with those shelves and then build the rest around them. I like to group books of similar sizes and colors together because they look best in those combinations. I also find that it is more interesting to mix up the arrangement of the books from one shelf to the next. The books might be standing on one shelf and lying flat on the next. As a separate option, we might have a mix of both on one shelf and then alternate which side the flat books are placed on from one shelf to the next. After you've placed your books, you will move on to placing the largest decorative objects since you may have some size limitations and fewer options for where these pieces can go.

"If you find yourself in a predicament in which your books are all different colors and don't work with your décor, but you need them in order to fill your shelves, you can turn all of your books' spines inward so that you see the pages instead."

Next, it is time to layer in smaller accessories. Accessories look great on top of a stack of books, but also work well in between stacks. If you collect a specific type of object, group them all together for maximum visual impact. If you scatter all of the objects, they no longer feel like a collection, so it is nice to have groupings of like things to help tell your story. For balance, follow the Pyramid Rule. When faced with a group of objects in varying sizes, arrange them in a way that mimics a pyramid with a peak and a taper. Using this method helps otherwise disparate items to feel more balanced to the eye and makes for much more interesting arrangements of objects. The finishing touch, and one of my favorite parts of styling bookcases, is adding in framed art. I find that it is an unexpected touch, especially when the art is casually leaning behind or on top of a stack of books. It is a great way to add color, character, and personality.

While we are on the topic of color, when I have a lot of books to choose from, I try to be mindful that the colors on the cover and spine of each book work with the overall décor of the space. For example, when we moved to our new house, one of the things I was most excited about was the fact that we have huge, built-in bookcases flanking the fireplace in our living room. However, because the décor in our living room is composed of a palette of black, white, and pink, I relegated a lot of books with brown, red, and orange colors to other rooms in the house because they clashed too much for me. Bookshelves provide a great opportunity for amplifying the color palette in a room. You can tie in a color from a pretty fabric in the room by wallpapering or painting the backs of the bookcases. If you find yourself in a predicament in which your books are all different colors and don't work with your décor, but you need them in order to fill your shelves, you can turn all of your books' spines inward so that you see the pages instead. The effect is modern and graphic, and solves the issue of books in colors that don't work with the overall design of your room!

This client had a ton of books. Since the colors of some of the spines didn't work with the color palette in their library, we turned the spines inward for a more neutral look.

DECORATING WITH MIRRORS

One of the signature elements of my work is using mirrors to punctuate a space. Not only will a beautiful mirror immediately increase the glamour quotient of any room, it is also a great way to cap off a chic vignette. Mirrors can be used pretty interchangeably with art, but is important to limit the number in a room.

Mirrors are great at the end of a hallway, above a console in an entryway, or over a sideboard in a dining room. One of my very favorite types of mirrors is a convex one. I tend to gravitate to convex mirrors because while they are reflective, the reflection is somewhat distorted,

Large mirrors can make a space appear more spacious as well as more glamorous.

making the effect less literal and more interesting. I have an oversized one above the fireplace in my living room and I absolutely love that it reflects the other side of the room and serves as a conversation piece because people rarely expect to see a big, convex mirror used that way.

Another way that I love to use mirrors is to find small convex mirrors, no more than eighteen inches in diameter and always with an interesting frame, and use them as the crowning piece in the uppermost part of a vignette in order to draw the eye up. I do this most often in bedrooms where we have a nightstand with a lamp on it, a piece of art hung above the nightstand, and then a few inches above the art, I add a small convex mirror. Not only does this technique raise the eye up, which is especially helpful if you have a tall headboard, it adds an unexpected touch of modern glamour. If you have a narrow wall near a dominant piece of art, this technique also works quite well because a piece of art and a mirror do not compete with one another in the way that two pieces or art or two mirrors would. In my dining room, I have three beautiful framed chinoiserie panels, which serve as the focal point of the space. The wall to the left of the panels opens onto the kitchen and has two smaller wall spaces on either side of the doorway where I have identical Lucite pedestals topped with blue-and-white chinoiserie jars. Can you guess what I hung above each jar? Eighteen-inch, Federal-style convex mirrors with gilded frames, of course!

Small, round mirrors are a great way to punctuate a vignette and draw the eye up.

In this bedroom, I did not want to cover up the beautiful wallpaper, but needed something to elevate the eye up toward the lovely canopy bed. A pair of gilt convex mirrors did just the trick.

I am not all that well versed in feng shui, but I have been told that it is not a good idea to place two mirrors directly across from one another, or to place a mirror in front of a window, because the energy gets trapped and bounces back and forth. That certainly doesn't sound like the ideal scenario, so I find myself abiding by that rule when placing mirrors in a space!

Following a carefully considered process is a lifesaver when designing your home. From having a functional floor plan and using timeless anchor pieces to creating a cohesive color palette and layering in art and accessories to add character and personality, having a plan and a process will help you make the best choices for you.

My best advice for you is to not bite off more than you can chew at any given moment. When working with a client, even when I am designing the entire house from top to bottom, I urge the client to share which elements are most important to them so that we can prioritize the project in phases. Doing so sets realistic and healthy expectations for everyone involved, ensures that we are on the same page, and makes the process so much more manageable and pleasant. Your home should be the place where you live your best life. Designing it to reflect the lifestyle you want for yourself is no small feat. I hope that my advice will make the process more enjoyable for you!

LIVE

Your personal style is universal in the sense that it transcends categories to tell the story of who you are. Your style is in the sofa silhouette you select and in the custom throw pillows that you put on it. It is in your choice of nail polish color and in your favorite perfume. Your style is in your choice between a loose, simple bouquet of flowers and a tight, artistic arrangement. It is in your go-to outfit and in your choice between vacationing in the mountains or on the beach. Style is in all of the choices you make, both conscious and subconscious, and how those choices come together to paint the picture of who you are. Once you've designed a beautiful home that reflects your style at its core, it is time to focus on the things you do within your home's walls that will help you to live your best life.

The round table in this elegant dining room lends itself to conversation between all guests.

CHAPTER SIX

EFFORTLESS ENTERTAINING

Now that you have designed the home you dreamed of and learned how to tell your story through the décor in your home as well as the way you dress, it is time to think about how to live your best life—your dolce vita. Most people would probably agree that the sweet life is all about surrounding yourself with the people you love, whether it's in your day-to-day life, on a special vacation, or when hosting beloved family and friends in your home.

Your style of entertaining, and most importantly, the way you make people feel while they are guests in your home, is a direct extension of your overall personal style. From the flowers you select for your dining table to the menu you create and the music you choose to play, all of these decisions help to set the mood for the occasion and send a loud and clear message about who you are and what makes you tick. The trick is to have fun, or at least look like you are having fun, while you do it. After all, have you ever been to a party where the hostess was obviously panicked or seemed put out by having people in her home and thought to yourself, "Well, this is fabulous"? I highly doubt it! Effortless entertaining is all about putting your guests at ease, making them feel special, and creating an experience they won't soon forget.

CREATING A GAME PLAN

If you tend to be detail-oriented, the idea of eliminating the stress of hosting a dinner or party may sound nearly impossible. The idea of preparing a meal, setting a beautiful table, and ensuring that everyone leaves with a full belly and having had a good time can seem daunting. However, if you plan far enough in advance and use some of my clever tips, entertaining at home can truly feel effortless.

1 Set a Date and Make a To-Do List

Everyone in my office knows that I am a notorious list maker. Making a list helps keep me on track and ensures that nothing falls through the cracks. Once you know the date of your event, put it on the calendar and begin planning all of the tasks you'll need to carry out in order to put on a successful event. The worst thing you could do is wait until the last minute and try to do everything the day of the event. Do not do this to yourself—it is pure torture!

2 Send an Invitation

A good rule of thumb for an event at your home is to give your guests somewhere in the ballpark of two to four weeks' notice. If you're celebrating a milestone birthday, you will likely have a date in mind pretty far in advance. For something more casual, like a dinner party, two weeks is plenty of notice for guests to plan accordingly. While you certainly don't have to design engraved invitations and send them in the mail, make things feel a bit more festive and special and send a chic digital invitation from Paperless Post to help set the mood for the event.

3 Ask about Food Allergies and Dietary Restrictions

In the age of dietary restrictions, food allergies, and food aversions, you will need to ensure that you are aware of any of your guests' food allergies or dietary restrictions in advance in order to have a suitable option for them. No one likes to feel like an overlooked afterthought! Be considerate of guests with dietary restrictions. Once you know what the various players are able to eat, you can plan your menu. If you are set on what you would like to serve, just be sure to have a suitable alternative for whoever has a food allergy or aversion.

4 Keep the Menu Simple

Over the years, I have found that even my most sophisticated friends crave simply prepared, comforting food. No one is going to come over expecting you to experiment with molecular gastronomy. Even Martha Stewart and Ina Garten know that if you keep the food simple, comforting, and tasty, and ensure that you have plenty of wine and cocktails on hand, everyone will leave feeling happy and satisfied!

5 Plan the Table Setting in Advance

Pick out your linens, dinnerware, flatware, and glasses in the early stages of your planning. If you have specific flowers in mind, order them from your florist or local grocery store in advance to ensure that they have the flowers you want on the day that you pick them up. I always find it best to set the table a day in advance so that it is ready to go and I have time to make any necessary tweaks.

When planning the furniture for your dining room, ensure that you have additional chairs for entertaining.
My table usually has six chairs, but there are two extra ones in the room for special occasions.

Live topiaries and
fresh flowers lend a
festive air—they're
a must when hosting
guests at my home!

Setting the table a day or two in advance is a good way to keep stress to
a minimum on the day of your event.

SETTING THE MENU FOR A STRESS-FREE DINNER PARTY

Not too long ago, while in Los Angeles for work, I was invited to an intimate dinner at the home of the founder of a huge company. She is a very successful businesswoman with incredible taste, so I found it incredibly charming when the dinner ended up being for ten people in her backyard. The food was perfect and simple. Her husband grilled chicken and salmon, there was a fabulous salad along with some simple veggies, and we had plenty of rosé and sparkling water. For dessert, she kept things stress-free and bought ice cream from a local ice cream shop that was all the rage in Los Angeles at that moment. Ice cream is a total crowd-pleaser and everyone was excited to try all of the creative flavors. That dinner has stuck with me because the simplicity and intimacy made it feel like such a special treat and allowed the hostess to spend quality time with each of her guests because she wasn't fussing over multiple courses of complicated food.

1 Keep It Simple
You don't have to serve your guests a complicated, elaborate meal in order to make them happy. Most people love simply prepared, beautifully presented food because it evokes a sense of comfort. Who doesn't love comfort food? I find that the combination of a salad, a grilled or roasted protein such as roasted chicken, grilled fish, or a roasted filet of beef, along with a vegetable, a starch, and a great dessert is always a crowd-pleaser.

2 Pick Tried-and-True Recipes
A dinner party or holiday is not a time to try out a recipe for something you have never made before. I have made this mistake in the past, and the stress of not knowing the recipe or how it will turn out is definitely not worth it.

3 Make a Little, Buy a Little
You don't have to make everything that you serve at a dinner party! With a little creativity, your guests will never know the difference. A cheese plate is a great appetizer and does not require cooking, just some assembly. You can pick up things like sides and desserts at a local specialty store or a bakery. Having these items taken care of will lessen the stress of getting everything ready.

4 Start Prepping Ahead of Time
In order to save time on the day of your event, think strategically about steps that you can take a day or two in advance. Have vegetables washed, measured, and chopped in advance, purchase the wine you plan to serve, and if you are making dessert yourself, you can usually do that at least a day in advance. Salads are easy to compose the morning of the event. Just make sure to wait to add the dressing until right before you are ready to serve it.

5 Prepare to Have a Great Time
Allow yourself plenty of time to get everything ready—including yourself—before your guests arrive. I like to pour myself a glass of wine before anyone comes in order to feel more at ease. Right before guests arrive, turn up the tunes, turn down the lights, and light candles to create ambiance. Be sure to greet your guests as soon as they come in and offer them a drink right away. No one wants to wait on a hostess who is still getting ready upstairs or who is knee-deep in a food crisis in the kitchen!

Moody cabinets painted
in Benjamin Moore's Hale
Navy and an antique
mirrored backsplash set
the party-ready tone
in this client's wet bar.

A LAST-MINUTE COCKTAIL PARTY

It can happen at the drop of a hat—you get a phone call from a friend who is in town and would love to come over to see you, or perhaps you're just feeling festive and are in the mood to celebrate something—a promotion, a birthday, or the fact that it's the end of the week! You can pull together an effortless last-minute cocktail party—arguably the easiest type of party to host, since it is generally pretty informal and you don't have to prepare an elaborate menu or set the table. If you make it a habit to keep most of these items stocked in your refrigerator and pantry at all times, you will be able to pull together a chic get-together at any given moment.

1 Pop the Bubbly
Technically, a cocktail party should have cocktails, but champagne is a crowd-pleaser. We always have a bottle chilling in our refrigerator along with plenty of wine in our pantry, so if we have unexpected company or cause for celebration, we can just pop a cork and get the party started.

2 Create a Signature Cocktail
Champagne or wine, beer, and a signature cocktail are all you truly need for a last-minute cocktail party. The former options are well liked by almost everyone and are ready to go right away. A signature cocktail makes any occasion feel special and keeps things simple so that you don't have to buy several different types of liquor along with a ton of various mixers and garnishes. In the warmer months, I love a gin southside or a margarita, while in the winter, a moscow mule is a definite crowd-pleaser.

3 Keep the Menu Simple
Be sure to keep a variety of lightly salted nuts in your pantry. They make a great, healthy snack, but are also the perfect thing to serve with drinks when you are in a pinch. Keep your refrigerator stocked with a wedge of Port Salut cheese, some colby jack cubes, and fresh fruit (grapes, strawberries, and figs pair beautifully with a variety of cheeses). Add some crackers and you can create a cheese platter in a jiffy.

4 Stock Your Freezer
A few well-chosen, frozen appetizers from Trader Joe's will keep in the freezer for a long time without taking up a lot of room and you can warm them up right before your guests arrive. Pigs in a blanket, anyone?

5 Set the Stage
Put some glasses and appetizer plates out on a pretty tray so that guests can help themselves to drinks and snacks. I always keep a variety of printed napkins in a drawer in my kitchen so I can use them when I don't want to go through the hassle of using linen napkins. If you don't have time to run to the store for flowers, be sure to at least burn a few candles and dim the lights for ambiance.

This room is ready for guests to arrive for a stylish brunch with pretty flowers and simple but delicious treats.

A STYLISH BRUNCH

A weekend brunch is a great time to entertain! Guests can come over and have a great time, then go home in time for everyone to enjoy the rest of the day. If you apply the same guidelines I outlined for a stress-free dinner party with a few tweaks, you can do most of the work ahead of time and host a fabulous brunch for your guests.

1 Make One Item from Scratch
As I mentioned before, you don't have to create a complicated, fussy menu to make your guests happy. Keep things simple by choosing a homemade dish that you can prepare in advance. For brunch, I love strata because you can make it in advance and then pop it in the oven before your guests arrive. It is egg based and can feature a great mix of proteins and veggies, so it is pretty and filling. A quiche is also a great option because you can make it the day before and it will reheat quite nicely.

2 Buy the Rest
Pair your strata or quiche with a simple green salad you can prepare in advance (buy a prewashed bag of spring mix to save time) and pick up a selection of pastries from a local bakery to round out the meal. You can do this the day before or in the morning before your guests arrive.

3 Set the Table
Create a pretty centerpiece for the table. If you are unsure about flowers, my favorite thing to do is choose one type of flower—maybe hydrangeas, tulips, or roses in one color—and arrange them in a simple vase. This is a timeless, classic, and foolproof way to create a flower arrangement. For a more formal meal, set the table with individual place settings. If you prefer to keep things more casual, set your dining table up like a buffet, with the different platters and serving pieces you plan to use, as well as plates, utensils, and napkins on one end of the table.

4 Pour the Drinks
Right before your guests arrive, make a big pitcher of mimosas or Bloody Marys for those who opt for alcohol with brunch. Champagne and rosé also pair rather nicely with brunch foods, but be sure to have plenty of coffee and plain orange juice on hand, too.

A custom-made tablecloth
in one of my favorite fabrics,
Schumacher's Samarkand
Ikat completely transforms
my dining room and sets the
stage for guest to arrive.

SETTING A BEAUTIFUL TABLE

I always find myself very inspired by
beautiful tabletops. It is so fun to see the
place settings other creative minds have
imagined. You certainly do not have to be
an entertaining maven with a limitless
supply of china, flatware, and linens to
set a lovely table. The key is to ensure
that you have a few options that are
appropriate for different seasons. I find
that rattan chargers or placemats are
quite versatile and can work with a blue-
and-white palette in the spring and
summer months, but also pair beautifully
with jewel tones in the fall. It is wonderful
if you have more than one set of flatware,
but you can certainly get a lot of mileage
out of one versatile pattern. The same
goes for your china, although it is nice to
have a simple set for daily use and more
casual occasions and a timeless set of
china for more formal gatherings.

A beautiful, properly set table helps to set the mood at dinner and ensures your guests have everything they need.

SALAD FORK

DINNER FORK

Linens are a fun and less expensive way of working additional options into your tabletop offerings. Don't forget to tie everything together with a beautiful, floral centerpiece, some candleholders, and hand-written place cards. Place cards are great because they eliminate the awkward moment where guests turn to the hostess to tell them where to sit. Plus, you can plan the seating arrangement ahead of time to ensure that people with similar interests are seated near one another in order to keep the conversation flowing and the energy alive. You can go the traditional route with paper place cards inscribed with each guest's name, or you can be a bit more creative and tie a little bouquet of fresh herbs with string and hang a tag on it; order decorated cookies to fit the theme of your event and have each guest's name written on their cookie with icing; or during the holidays, place a pretty ornament at each guest's place setting and hang an inscribed gift tag from it.

WINE

WATER

DINNER
KNIFE

SOUP
SPOON

DESSERT
SPOON

Every room needs
something living in it.
Flowers make every
space more beautiful.

IN BLOOM

One of my favorite reasons for entertaining is getting to deck out my house in beautiful flowers. Truth be told, I buy fresh flowers at the store during almost all of my weekly grocery runs. Unless I know that I will be traveling most of the week, it is pretty safe to assume that I will have fresh flowers in my house. It is a small luxury that brings me a lot of joy and truly makes a difference in making my house feel like our home. Why limit flowers to a special occasion when one can have plenty of festive flowers around every day?

When it comes to flowers, I apply the same theory of effortless entertaining to the task. Of course, I love the stunning floral arrangements crafted by my favorite local florist, and I certainly don't profess to be a floral design pro, but I have a good eye, I know what I like, and I know a few simple tricks that allow me to create beautiful arrangements simply and inexpensively.

Fresh-cut pink hydrangea from the garden are the perfect addition to this bedroom in the Hamptons.

A STEP-BY-STEP GUIDE FOR FOOLPROOF FLOWERS

1 Stock Up on Vessels

The two things I find most surprising when I am styling someone's house for a photo shoot are a lack of books and a lack of vases and vessels for flowers. Granted, I am bordering on hoarder levels for both of these items, but it is generally a good idea to make sure you have a variety of vases in various styles, widths, and heights, including a few staples. I like to have a combination of glass cylinder vases—low ones for flowers like hydrangeas, roses, and peonies and tall ones for branches, delphinium, sunflowers, and bells of Ireland. It is also a good idea to have a variety of bud vases in both glass and ceramic to place on bedside tables, end tables, bathroom vanities, entry tables, and so on. They are super versatile! Lastly, mix in some cool pottery, elegant mint julep cups, blue-and-white vases, and metallic vessels to dress up your arrangements.

2 Know Your Color Palette

In my own house, I prefer white and green flowers, along with blooms in various shades of pink. Not only are these among my favorite colors for flowers, they also complement the décor in my house. Think about the colors in your home when deciding which types of flowers to purchase. For instance, red, yellow, and orange flowers are pretty, but they would clash with the overall color palette in my house. When designing the flowers for each of my clients' homes, I keep the colors in the room in mind when selecting the flowers and I keep things simple by ensuring that the blooms in each arrangement are all the same color or complement each other nicely.

3 Setting the Foundation

More often than not, I stick to a single bloom in an arrangement. Selecting one type of flower in a single color, placed in a tasteful vessel, always looks chic and appropriate. However, when I am feeling more adventurous or have a variety of flowers to work with, I start with the larger flowers, such as hydrangea first, and arrange them in the vase. Next, I add in accent flowers, such as roses in the same color or a complementary shade. Lastly, I fill in any gaps with some filler courtesy of some verdant leaves or wispy flowers such as freesia or lisianthus to make the arrangement feel lush.

4 Extend the Life of your Flowers

Over the years, I have learned from various floral experts that you can in fact extend the lifespan of your flowers. Begin by asking if the flowers you have selected prefer cold or warm water. Ensure that the vases you are using are clean. Dirty vases are not only unsightly, but they harbor harmful bacteria that can cut the life of your flowers short. Add flower food to the vase as you fill it with water, then cut the stems of the flowers at a diagonal. After you have arranged your flowers, if you notice the water getting a bit murky after a few days, change it and give your flowers another snip on the ends so that they start drinking again. Flowers can seem finicky, but I have had cut hydrangeas last over ten days by following these tips in the past!

FLORAL ABCS

Anemone

Flowers are one of the simplest pleasures in life. I love them and always find that a house comes alive when it is filled with beautiful blooms and pretty plants. I rarely make it out of the grocery store without a few bunches of flowers. If it is peony season, which happens between May and late June, there is a strong probability that I will purchase more than my fair share anytime I happen upon them, even if I already have some at home. I find that arranging them at home is relaxing and I get to enjoy their beauty for several days. Since I am not a florist, I generally keep things simple and stick to my favorite flowers.

Hydrangea

ANEMONE
BEGONIA
CAMELLIA
DAHLIA
ENGLISH ROSE
FREESIA
GARDENIA
HYDRANGEA
ICELAND POPPIES
JASMINE

LILY OF THE VALLEY
MAGNOLIA
NARCISSUS
ORCHID
PEONY
QUEEN ANNE'S LACE
RANUNCULUS
SWEET PEA
TULIP
VIBURNUM
ZINNIA

Orchid

I love having fresh flowers in my house whenever possible. Here, you'll find my favorite flowers from A to Z. (Illustrations by Inslee Fariss)

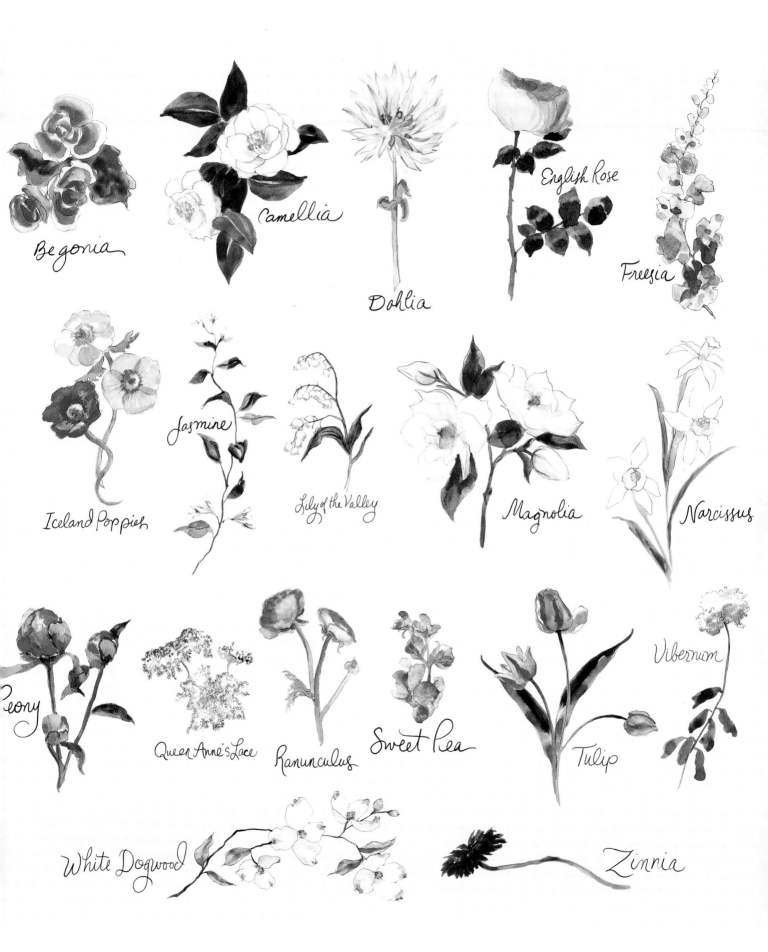

Begonia

Camellia

Dahlia

English Rose

Freesia

Iceland Poppies

Jasmine

Lily of the Valley

Magnolia

Narcissus

Peony

Queen Anne's Lace

Ranunculus

Sweet Pea

Tulip

Viburnum

White Dogwood

Zinnia

Fresh flowers and
a carafe of water set a
welcoming tone
in my guest bedroom.

"I want my guests, whether they are in my home for dinner or for an entire weekend, to feel welcome, comfortable, and relaxed."

BE MY GUEST

A wise woman once said that a host should spend a night in his or her guest bedroom in order to ensure that everything is comfortable enough for a guest. From a design perspective, guest bedrooms, like powder rooms, are a great way to experiment with bolder design choices. If there is a wallpaper or paint color you absolutely love, but are afraid it would be too much to commit to in a room you use every day, a guest bedroom might be the perfect place for it, since it probably won't get as much use as the other rooms in your house and your guests are likely to appreciate a room with panache. My guest bedroom is more pattern-driven than any other room in the house for this very reason. I dressed the space in various patterns in blue and white and even opted for printed fabric lamp shades. The room is cozy and fun!

I love hosting overnight guests. I derive a lot of joy from preparing our guest bedroom for visiting friends and family. I want my guests, whether they are in my home for dinner or for an entire weekend, to feel welcome, comfortable, and relaxed. I do my best to make sure that guests know they are welcome to help themselves to whatever they like by doing things such as leaving a few bowls, glasses, and napkins on the kitchen counter before they arrive and placing a glass carafe filled with water on the nightstand. Providing your guests with adequate space, comfortable surroundings, and the essentials they need will instantly make them feel welcome.

My guest bedroom features comfortable bedding and all of the essentials to ensure a comfortable stay for friends and family.

Guest Room Essentials
- Fresh flowers on the nightstand
- A carafe filled with water and a glass for drinking
- Extra blankets
- An assortment of pillows (I have both down and down alternative pillows on the bed in our guest room so that guests can choose what they prefer)
- A luggage rack
- Plenty of empty hangers
- Nice soap
- Shampoo and conditioner
- Moisturizing body wash
- Ibuprofen and antacids in the bathroom cabinet
- A spare toothbrush and toothpaste
- Cotton balls and cotton swabs
- Interesting books and local magazines
- A phone charger
- A handwritten welcome note with the Wi-Fi password

Pattern play and
stacks of books
make for a cheerful
guest bedroom.

"Be a gracious host by giving your guests flexibility, but remember that it is your job to ensure that they have a nice time while staying with you."

A few days before your guest is set to arrive, check in with them regarding any desired snacks and drinks. If I know that a friend likes a certain snack, prefers a specific cereal in the morning, or enjoys a glass of rosé before dinner every evening, I make sure to have those items on hand for their stay. Another important thing to note when you are hosting overnight guests is to have a plan. Be considerate and check in with them regarding their plans while they are in town, particularly if they are staying with you while in town for a work commitment. Be flexible, but plan a few activities in advance to make sure that you are never at a loss for what to do. We once spent a holiday weekend with someone who literally didn't have a thing planned for us to do and we felt like an afterthought and the trip felt like a total waste of time. If you have specific dinner plans during their stay, be sure to let them know ahead of time so that they can plan to attend and dress accordingly. Be a gracious host by giving your guests flexibility, but remember that it is your job to ensure that they have a nice time while staying with you.

Light streams
through the
windows of this
cozy bedroom.

The color palette
in this pretty
bedroom is tied
together with
various pale blue
accents from
the headboard and
lumbar pillow
to the lamp and
bud vase.

HOSTESS GIFTS WITH STYLE

While it is important to be a good host, it is even more important to be a good guest. Whether I have been invited to a friend's home for dinner or for the weekend, I do my best to get there on time and in good spirits. It is bad to be late, but it is even worse to surprise your host and show up early! I make an effort to be considerate by being in the moment. There are few things as impolite as being glued to your phone when your host has gone to great lengths to have you as a guest in their home. It should go without saying, but I treat my friends' homes with the same consideration and respect that I would want them to show my home. As an overnight guest, I make my bed before leaving my room each morning and ensure that I keep my room as neat as possible, returning everything to the way it was presented to me when I arrived. Lastly, I always send a thank-you. Depending on the occasion and your relationship, sometimes a handwritten, heartfelt thank-you will suffice. Other times, you'll want to do a little more to show your appreciation.

These are just a few of my favorite gifts to give—and receive. Hint, hint!

- A beautiful coffee table book
- A stack of old issues of the original *House & Garden* or *Domino*
- A scented candle
- Your favorite cookbook
- A potted orchid or myrtle topiary
- A floral arrangement—if this is for a friend in another city, ask for a florist recommendation. There's nothing worse than an expensive floral delivery that is lackluster at best.

- A box of fresh gardenias from High Camp Supply
- A bottle of wine from your favorite winery
- Sweets for your sweet: I love DeLuscious Cookies in Los Angeles. They ship nationwide and their cookies are insanely delicious! Sprinkles Cupcakes are a crowd favorite, while Jeni's Ice Cream in Ohio allows you to ship a sampler of ice cream pints to friends nationwide.

One of my favorite hostess gifts to give is a beautiful book. As you can tell from my bedroom, I have quite a few myself!

Tastemakers' Go-To Hostess Gifts

- **Vicente Wolf** An orchid in a clay pot
- **Tori Mellott** Monogrammed tea towels
- **Alyssa Kapito** The Ernesto Candle by Cire Trudon
- **John Robshaw** A turban—she probably does not have one
- **Lauren Liess** Something from my garden
- **Nam Dang Mitchell** What's wrong with wine? Nothing!
- **Alessandra Branca** A vintage book
- **Suzanne Tucker** McEvoy Ranch olive oil
- **Brian McCarthy** Turquoise or amethyst glassware from Gilmor Glass
- **Kristen Buckingham** Tequila
- **Bunny Williams** Homemade cookies
- **India Hicks** A baby pineapple that can sit as a decorative object, then be eaten when it is fully mature.
- **Susan Feldman** A vintage lassi cup or a mint julep cup with a lottery ticket inside of it

A mix of meaningful art
and touches of my favorite
colors make my bedroom
feel personal and special.

LIVING LA DOLCE VITA

Your home is your respite from the rest of the world. It is where you should feel the greatest sense of safety and peace. Not only is it an outward reflection of who you are at your very core, but it also sends a clear message to the world about what truly matters to you. Your home sets the stage for the type of life you want to live. You may not know exactly what that means when you initially set out to transform your house into your home, but I hope that the advice I have shared serves as a reminder that it is okay for things to take a little longer than planned in order to get things right in the end. Sometimes, in design as in love, it pays to hold out for "the one," even if the one is the perfect piece of art, a vintage chair, or a beautiful antique mirror. Your home and everything in it should give you a sense of joy. Remember that and be faithful to your taste, eschew trends in favor of classic pieces, and trust the process. Go out and live your dolce vita!

ABOUT THE AUTHOR

Paloma Contreras is an award-winning interior decorator, tastemaker, and design blogger based in Houston, Texas. Paloma's design sensibility is a modern take on traditional style, gravitating toward classic silhouettes and timeless pieces paired with a touch of glamour and an infusion of color. Paloma has honed her distinct eye for style through nearly a decade in the design industry and a lifetime of appreciating beauty in all of its various forms. Paloma is well versed in a broad range of styles, which are executed in a manner that is polished, refined, and effortless. Paloma launched her widely read blog, *La Dolce Vita*, in 2007 where she continues to write about "the sweet life" on a daily basis. She has amassed a loyal following of design enthusiasts who turn to her for the latest and greatest in design, fashion, and luxury travel.

Paloma has been recognized as a "Next Wave" interior designer by *House Beautiful*, is one of *Luxe* magazine's "New Guard" list of 10 Designers to Know, and was recently named on *Elle Décor*'s prestigious A-List. Paloma is also #4 on *Forbes*'s list of the Top 10 Social Media Influencers in the Home category. Paloma believes that the most beautiful interiors are also the most personal.

RESOURCES

ART

Alexis Walter
www.alexiswalterart.com
Arftully Walls
www.artfullywalls.com
Catherine B. Jones
www.catherinejonesstudio.com
Kayce Hughes
www.kaycehughes.com
Lindsey J. Porter
www.lindseyjporter.com
Natural Curiosities
www.naturalcuriosities.com
Serena & Lily
www.serenaandlily.com
Soicher Marin
www.soicher-marin.com
Wendover Art
www.wendoverart.com
William McLure
www.williammclure.com

BOUTIQUE

À Bientôt
www.abientot713.com
AREA
www.area-houston.com
Blue Print
www.blueprintstore.com
Bungalow Classic
www.bungalowclassic.com
Circa Interiors & Antiques
www.circainteriors.com
Found
www.foundforthehome.com
Harbinger
www.harbingerla.com
Hollywood at Home
www.hollywoodathome.com
Huff Harrington
www.huffharrington.com
James Showroom
www.jamesshowroom.com
John Rosselli & Associates
www.johnrosselli.com
Lam Bespoke
www.lambespoke.com
Lynn Goode Vintage
www.lynngoodevintage.com
Mecox Gardens
www.mecoxgardens.com
Thompson + Hanson
www.thompsonhanson.com

FABRICS & WALLPAPER

Brunschwig & Fils
www.brunschwig.com
Cole & Son
www.cole-and-son.com
DeGournay
www.degournay.com
Duralee
www.duralee.com
Holland & Sherry
www.hollandandsherry.com
Holly Hunt
www.hollyhunt.com
John Robshaw
www.johnrobshaw.com
Katie Leede
www.katieleede.com
Katie Ridder
www.katieridder.com
Kravet
www.kravet.com
Lee Jofa
www.leejofa.com
Lisa Fine
www.lisafinetextiles.com
Michael S. Smith
www.michaelsmithinc.com
Perennials
www.perennialsfabrics.com
Peter Dunham Textiles
www.peterdunhamtextiles.com
Phillip Jeffries
www.phillipjeffries.com
Scalamandré
www.scalamandre.com
Schumacher
www.fschumacher.com
Thibaut
www.thibautdesign.com
Zak + Fox
www.zakandfox.com

FURNITURE

Ave Home
www.avehome.com
Bernhardt
www.bernhardt.com
Bungalow 5
www.bungalow5.com
Century Furniture
www.centuryfurniture.com
Charles Stewart
www.charlesstewartcompany.com
Henredon
www.henredon.com
Hickory Chair
www.hickorychair.com
Highland House
www.highlandhousefurniture.com
Lee Industries
www.leeindustries.com
Made Goods
www.madegoods.com
Mr. & Mrs. Howard for Sherrill
www.sherrillfurniture.com
Noir
www.noirfurniturela.com
Stanley Furniture
www.stanleyfurniture.com
Tara Shaw Maison
www.tarashaw.com
The New Traditionalists
www.thenewtraditionalists.com
Worlds Away
www.worlds-away.com

HARDWARE

LuxHoldUps
www.etsy.com/shop/luxholdups
Rejuvenation
www.rejuvenation.com
Restoration Hardware
www.restorationhardware.com
Rocky Mountain Hardware
www.rockymountainhardware.com
Waterworks
www.waterworks.com

LIGHTING

Christopher Spitzmiller
www.christopherspitzmiller.com
Circa Lighting
www.circalighting.com
Coleen & Company
www.coleenandcompany.com
Jonathan Browning
www.jonathanbrowninginc.com
Julie Neill Designs
www.julieneill.com
Visual Comfort
www.visualcomfort.com

LINENS

Biscuit
www.biscuit-home.com
John Robshaw
www.johnrobshaw.com
Leontine Linens
www.leontinelinens.com
Matouk
www.matouk.com
Peacock Alley
www.peacockalley.com
Serena & Lily
www.serenaandlily.com

NATIONAL STORES

Anthropologie
www.anthropologie.com
CB2
www.cb2.com
Crate & Barrel
www.crateandbarrel.com
Design Within Reach
www.dwr.com
Pottery Barn
www.potterybarn.com
Room & Board
www.roomandboard.com
West Elm
www.westelm.com
Williams Sonoma Home
www.wshome.com
Wisteria
www.wisteria.com

ONLINE

1stdibs
www.1stdibs.com
Arianna Belle
www.ariannabelle.com
Ballard Designs
www.ballarddesigns.com
Chairish
www.chairish.com
Dering Hall
www.deringhall.com
Etsy
www.etsy.com
One Kings Lane
www.onekingslane.com
The Mine
www.themine.com
Viyet
www.viyet.com

CREDITS

PAINT

Benjamin Moore
www.benjaminmoore.com
Farrow & Ball
us.farrow-ball.com
Sherwin-Williams
www.sherwinwilliams.com

PLUMBING

Kallista
www.kallista.com
Kohler
www.kohler.com
Rejuvenation
www.rejuvenation.com
Restoration Hardware
www.restorationhardware.com
Waterworks
www.waterworks.com

RUGS

Dash & Albert
www.dashandalbert.com
Merida
www.meridastudio.com
Rug Mart
www.rugmarthouston.com
Stark Carpet
www.starkcarpet.com

STONE & TILE

Caesarstone
www.caesarstoneus.com
Walker Zanger
www.walkerzanger.com
Ann Sacks
www.annsacks.com
Daltile
www.daltile.com

Chic Combinations: Fabrics (page 77)
CLASSIC GLAMOUR (*left to right*): Arianna Belle: Leopard Velvet; Arianna Belle: Champagne Velvet; Arianna Belle: White with Black Greek Key Trim
MODERN TRADITIONAL (*left to right*): Lee Jofa: Hummingbirds in Cream; Arianna Belle: Olive Green Velvet; F. Schumacher: Betwixt
ECLECTIC COOL (*left to right*): F. Schumacher: Pyne Hollyhock in Charcoal; Arianna Belle: Peacock Velvet; Brunschwig & Fils: Les Touches in Black
CASUAL CHIC (*left to right*): F. Schumacher: Indian Arbre in Hyacinth; Arianna Belle: Powder Blue Velvet; Quadrille: Java Java in Navy

Chic Combinations: Lighting (page 90)
CEILING (*left to right*): Natalya Chandelier by John Rosselli for Visual Comfort; Calais Chandelier by Niermann Weeks for Visual Comfort; Sommerard Large Chandelier by AERIN for Visual Comfort; Farlane Small Chandelier by Thomas O'Brien for Visual Comfort
WALL (*left to right*): Lucy Wall Sconce by John Rosselli for Visual Comfort; Jacqueline Medium Sconce by AERIN for Visual Comfort; Melange Sconce by Kelly Wearstler for Visual Comfort; Venice Sconce by Thomas O'Brien for Visual Comfort
TABLE (*left to right*): Deauville Table Lamp by E.F. Chapman for Visual Comfort; Juliette Table Lamp by Suzanne Kasler for Visual Comfort; Olsen Table Lamp by AERIN for Visual Comfort; Hargett Buffet Lamp by J. Randall Powers for Visual Comfort
FLOOR (*left to right*): Parish Floor Lamp by Thomas O'Brien for Visual Comfort; Riga Floor Lamp by AERIN for Visual Comfort; Clarkson Triple Floor Lamp by AERIN for Visual Comfort; Longacre Floor Lamp by Thomas O'Brien for Visual Comfort

Chic Combinations: The Kitchen (page 113)
CLASSIC GLAMOUR (*left to right*): Cabinet Color: Benjamin Moore: Black Beauty; Countertop: Caesarstone: Statuario Maximus; Faucet: Waterworks: Three Hole Gooseneck Kitchen Faucet; Cabinet Hardware: Waterworks: Henry 4" Pull; Lighting: Visual Comfort: Morris Large Lantern by Suzanne Kasler
MODERN TRADITIONAL (*left to right*): Cabinet Color: Benjamin Moore: Revere Pewter; Countertop: Caesarstone: Piatra Grey; Faucet: Waterworks: Julia One Hole High Profile Kitchen Faucet; Cabinet Hardware: Waterworks: Boulevard 1.5" Knob; Lighting: Visual Comfort: Lily Hanging Shade by Alexa Hampton

ECLECTIC COOL (*left to right*): Cabinet Color: Benjamin Moore: Hale Navy; Countertop: Caesarstone: Montblanc; Faucet: Waterworks: Regular Gooseneck Double Spout Marquee Kitchen Faucet; Cabinet Hardware: Waterworks: R.W. Atlas 1.5" Knob; Lighting: Visual Comfort: Precision Large Pendant by Kelly Wearstler
CASUAL CHIC (*left to right*): Cabinet Color: Benjamin Moore: White Dove; Countertop: Caesarstone: London Grey; Faucet: Waterworks: Easton Classic Two Hole Bridge Gooseneck Kitchen Faucet; Cabinet Hardware: Waterworks: Paragon 4.25" Pull; Lighting: Visual Comfort: Bryden Medium Round Pendant by E.F. Chapman

Chic Combinations: The Powder Room (page 133)
CLASSIC GLAMOUR (*left to right*): Wallpaper: Beaujeu by AERIN for Lee Jofa; Vanity: Waterworks: Demi Lune Wood Three Leg Washstand; Faucet: Waterworks: Isla High Profile Lavatory Faucet; Mirrors: Wisteria: French Mirror; Lighting: Visual Comfort: Eaton Sconce by AERIN
MODERN TRADITIONAL (*left to right*): Wallpaper: Les Touches by Brunschwig & Fils; Vanity: Waterworks: Henry Metal Single Two Leg Washstand; Faucet: Waterworks: Henry Gooseneck Lavatory Faucet; Mirrors: Wisteria: Pagoda Mirror; Lighting: Visual Comfort: Bryant Sconce by Thomas O'Brien
ECLECTIC COOL (*left to right*): Wallpaper: Graffito by Kelly Wearstler for Groundworks; Vanity: Waterworks: Arden Single Washstand; Faucet: Waterworks: Henry Wall Mounted Lavatory Faucet; Mirrors: Wisteria: Scallop Edge Mirror; Lighting: Visual Comfort: Melange Pill Form Sconce by Kelly Wearstler
CASUAL CHIC (*left to right*): Wallpaper: La Fiorentina by David Hicks for GP & J Baker; Vanity: Waterworks: Worth Single Wood Vanity; Faucet: Waterworks: Henry Gooseneck Lavatory Faucet with Teak Cylinders; Mirrors: Wisteria: Moroccan Mirror; Lighting: Visual Comfort: Elkins Sconce by Thomas O'Brien

ACKNOWLEDGMENTS

As they say, it takes a village, and this book is no exception. I am so grateful for the most incredible team.

To my literary agent, Berta Treitl, I couldn't have done this without you. Thank you for your vision, encouragement, and guidance. You are the best teammate I could have asked for.

To my editor, Rebecca Kaplan—working with you was a dream. Thank you for your insight and your faith in me. To the entire team at Abrams, I am so proud to be a part of the Abrams family. You create the most inspiring books through your dedication and brilliance.

To my graphic designer, Emily Wardwell, thank you for making this book even more beautiful than I could have imagined. I wanted to work with you from the moment I decided to write a book. Thank you for sharing your amazing talent and good taste.

I was so fortunate to work with some incredible photographers for this project. To Brittany Ambridge, thank you for the beautiful images you captured of my New Orleans project. I love knowing that it lives on through your lens. To Max Burkhalter, thank you for lending your immense talent to this project. You captured the true spirit of each of these special homes. Thank you for bringing your positive energy to every shoot!

To my wonderful clients, thank you for allowing me into your homes and your lives. It is my true honor and privilege to design your beautiful houses to reflect the way you want them to feel and function. Thank you for your trust and for allowing me to live out my dream each day. To those of you whose homes appear in the pages of this book, I am eternally grateful.

To my amazing Paloma Contreras Design team—Ashton Marshall, Devon Liedtke, Amanda Tharp, and Mary Kate Carl, you keep the wheels moving! There are not enough words to describe how thankful I am for your hard work and dedication. You are each so talented and inspire me on a daily basis. Thank you for always finding a way to make me laugh. Teamwork makes the dream work!

To Elizabeth Blitzer, Liza Morten Gioia, Nan Philip, and Bobby Graham, thank you for your support, encouragement, and enthusiasm. I am so grateful for all that you do.

In this elegant living room, timeless art and classic silhouettes comingle with a modern Lucite cocktail table.

To my dear blog readers, your readership and support over the years has inspired me beyond measure. This book was possible because you allowed me into your lives each day. *La Dolce Vita* has been the source of so many incredible things in my life—friendships with people I respect and admire and access to wonderful mentors—and it has opened the doors that have empowered me to change the entire course of my career. It has given me the courage and skills I needed in order to chase after my dreams and has not only given me the opportunity to connect with so many inspiring people, it has also been a catalyst for personal and professional growth for which I will be forever grateful. Thank you for being such an important part of my life.

To my family, thank you for always encouraging me to dream big and for cheering me on along the way. Your support means the world to me. I love you.

To my friends, you inspire me beyond measure. Thank you for your love, generosity of spirit, and support. Mark Sikes, Lauren Liess, Alyssa Kapito, Young Huh, and Alberto Villalobos—thank you for being my sounding board.

Last, but most certainly not least—to my incredible husband, Fabian. You are my world. Thank you for the beautiful life we share. You've been by my side during every step of this journey. Thank you for believing in me and loving me the way you do. There is no better partner than you. And to my sweet puppy son, Tate—you converted me into a true animal lover. You taught me how to love in a way I didn't know was possible.

Editor: Rebecca Kaplan
Designer: Emily Wardwell
Production Manager: Mike Kaserkie

Library of Congress Control Number: 2017956795

ISBN: 978-1-4197-2983-6
eISBN: 978-1-68335-320-1

Front cover: Brittany Ambridge
Back cover: Max Burkhalter
Southern Style Now Bedroom Photos
(pages 6, 192–193): Brittany Ambridge
All Other Photos: Max Burkhalter
Illustrations by Inslee Fariss

Cover © 2018 Abrams

Printed and bound in the United States
10 9 8 7 6 5 4 3 2 1

Abrams books are available at special discounts
when purchased in quantity for premiums and
promotions as well as fundraising or educational
use. Special editions can also be created to
specification. For details, contact specialsales@
abramsbooks.com or the address below.

ABRAMS The Art of Books
195 Broadway, New York, NY 10007
abramsbooks.com